Building Hope

GABRIELLE KALLUS

Gotham Books

30 N Gould St.
Ste. 20820, Sheridan, WY 82801
https://gothambooksinc.com/

Phone: 1 (307) 464-7800

© 2025 *Gabrielle Kallus*. All rights reserved.

No part of this book may be reproduced, stored in a retrieval system, or transmitted by any means without the written permission of the author.

Published by Gotham Books (March 27, 2025)

ISBN: 979-8-3492-4075-1 (P)
ISBN: 979-8-3492-4076-8 (E)

Because of the dynamic nature of the Internet, any web addresses or links contained in this book may have changed since publication and may no longer be valid.

The views expressed in this work are solely those of the author and do not necessarily reflect the views of the publisher, and the publisher hereby disclaims any responsibility for them.

Dedicated especially to my children,
John, Patrick, and Jacob,
My family,
And my best friend and supporter,
One of my first teachers in life,
Patty Hirsch.
She alone knows all I have gone through!
And to all those who have been here
Through both the struggles
And the good times as well.

Table of Contents

Table of Contents v
Foreword 1 vii
Foreword 2 xi
Learning How to Fly 1
Personal Stories 3
Positivity Defined 11
Purpose, Motivation, Faith, and Belief 18
Confidence and Courage 27
Perseverance, Determination, Endurance and Patience 33
Conquering Fear 42
Gratitude and Thankfulness 47
The Search for Meaning in Life 52
Negative Thinking 59
Prayer 68
Love and Acceptance 76
Depression, Anxiety, and Loneliness 84
Facing Challenges 94
Afterward 100
Bibliography 102

Foreword 1

People are like stained-glass windows; they sparkle and shine when the sun is out, but when the darkness sets in their true beauty is revealed only if there is a light within.

Elizabeth Kubler-Ross

In September, 1976, I was teaching Kindergarten at Sacred Heart School in Hallettsville, Texas. A very distraught mother came in to speak with me about her daughter, Gabby. Knowing all moms want the very best for their children, this mother shared her fears and genuine concerns regarding her child's learning capacity. This family had been involved in a tragic vehicle accident 3 years earlier, and Gabby was thrown out of the vehicle through the windshield. She suffered significant brain damage and was transferred to a Houston hospital by ambulance. As a result of her injuries, it was necessary for Gabby to relearn many of the basic functions of a child her age. Walking, talking, and other sensory tasks were on this agenda. Her mom was fearful that Gabby might not be able to function in the classroom.

I agreed to meet with Gabby the next day, and hadn't a clue what to expect of this small child. Gabby walked in wearing her adorable lion pinafore and had the biggest smile on her face. She appeared to be very comfortable in the classroom, overjoyed to check out everything on display in the room. After watching in amazement and visiting with her, I knew Gabby would do well in kindergarten. I promised to give her extra help if she needed it. Although a bit shy, she was always cheerful and eager to learn something new each day. She was incredibly kind to her classmates and worried about them if they were sad or confused. Even at age 5, she was a very confident child. She remained positively radiant!

Over the years as Gabby and I crossed paths, I saw that she had remained steadfast in her zest for life. Even though school was becoming more challenging and social situations more intense, she maintained that persevering, confident, and motivated attitude as always. Now more mature, Gabby relied on her faith in God to guide her through the major decisions of her life.

Following high school, Gabby remained optimistic about her future and was persistent in reaching her goals and dream. Some years after receiving her Bachelor's degree, she pushed forward determined to achieve in grad school and received her Master's degree. This proved challenging at times because she now had 3 young sons under foot, but her patience and determination overcame her frustration. We would often meet up at Walmart and she would update me on her progress. Gabby reaffirmed her self-confidence by receiving her Master's degree in psychology.

In our life's journey, we all encounter tribulations of one sort or another, and we must learn to navigate through these stumbling blocks. Over the past few years Gabby has had her share of sharp rocks. She has had to struggle with disappointments and heart wrenching losses. Her perseverance in the wake of these difficulties has been no less than admirable. Although sometimes saddened and perplexed by her own personal agonies, Gabby has relied on God to give her peace, strength, and assurance to move forward. She has never stopped believing in what God can do and has remained positive that everything will work out in God's timing.

In spite of Gabby's difficulties, I am always amazed at her relationship towards others. She willingly places the lives of others ahead of herself, reaching out in compassion and genuine concern to those around her. Her incredible love shines through her like a beacon, her nurturing disposition encouraging others to persevere and believe in themselves. Her comforting smile and joyful light-hearted laughter can warm the souls of many a person.

Gabby does not dwell glumly on her problems. She continues to demonstrate her positive outlook on life. She stays vigilant with the assurance that patience, prayer, and determination will provide her with the peace to move forward. Gabby certainly reflects that pure light from within.

Patty Hirsch

Foreword 2

Life is not easy. No one has gotten through life without a meaningful challenge or two. You and I have both had struggles in life. These struggles can range from mental and physical struggles, to emotional and spiritual difficulties. Because we can have such a wide variety of struggles, it becomes important to not only understand where they are coming from, but also to learn different ways to cope and effectively get through each struggle. It is how we respond to these challenges that shows others the person that we truly are.

I have had many struggles, both external and internal, physical and mental. It is how we respond to these challenges that show others the person that we are. When I first began writing this book in January 2018, I had been in a really dark place mentally. My children had just moved in with my younger sister because I had some legal problems come up. Then my mom passed away and not even a week after her funeral I was arrested and taken to jail. I was unable to take the original writing with me, but while in jail for those four months, I wrote this book for a couple of reasons. First, I had to do something active. Second, I needed to write a book about positivity because it was what I needed at that time. The Bible verses in this book are the ones that helped me in those four months. So, this book is meant to be uplifting as well as therapeutic. In times of struggle I still turn to the pages here because it helps me to remember that through all the struggles there is hope, and building hope is what this book is all about.

In 1973 I sustained a traumatic brain injury. As a result, the doctors at that time did not believe that I would be able to lead a productive life. They felt that it was likely that I would live in a vegetative state for the rest of my life, or have too many obstacles stacked against me to lead a productive life.

During my hospitalization I had three near death experiences. Each time I was told to "Go back." Even though the doctors did not seem to hold out hope for a productive life, these experiences gave my parents hope that maybe I would be able to go farther in life. My mother, especially, believed that my survival meant that I had a God-given purpose in life. My parents believed that I would be able to achieve many things. They worked with me to relearn the basic skills of walking, talking, and the many other skills I would need

How did I begin to even understand the reasons behind the struggles? How did I get past them? I began by considering the challenges that had been bestowed upon me. Because I had survived a traumatic brain injury that no one considered able to survive, I knew that my life could become extremely difficult. What did I do to get past the difficulties? I worked at building various skills, such as walking, reading, swimming, and doing various puzzles as well as games that would challenge my mind. My mother, especially, would tell me that I survived for a reason, and that I had a purpose. I believed this as well.

How did I get past the many challenges I have had? First, I found meaning through the struggles. I found that my faith, my belief in a higher being and praying for His guidance served the purpose of calming my "inner demons," the voices that would tell me that I was no good or unworthy of love and acceptance.

This book will help you learn ways to help you remain positive in the negative times of your life. Hope and positivity are not easy to come by, as many times struggles come up that make us doubt ourselves. My most recent challenge included jail time, but I have had many other struggles as well throughout the years. This book includes many things that have helped me to get and maintain a positive attitude, personal experiences, and Biblical passages that have helped us to get our minds focused on what we need to do. Also included are poems written by the author, poems of encouragement that I hope will help you to understand that attitude is everything!

Developing a positive outlook can be simplified. I hope that through reading this book, you are able to get out of the funk that you have been in. Maintaining positivity even through challenging times is possible! It is easy to stay negative, but a positive attitude will allow you to accomplish more than you ever thought possible!

Learning How to Fly

Seagulls flying amongst the wind

All in flight—except for one on the shore.

The one on the shore is the one that,

With help from friends,

Will only learn to stretch his wings

And learn to fly up to the sky

And will have a beautiful wingspan.

The seagull never tried to fly,

And so he never learned.

He was a mature-looking bird

That ne'er learned how to fly,

Or to stretch his limits,

To cry.

Though old, he never learned how to fly

And go beyond the limits,

Go toward the sky.

Back in 1988, when I wrote this poem, I was struggling with life, not knowing what I wanted to do. I had no idea what my purpose was, and I felt isolated. I was at a point where depression had set in. The writing of this poem made me realize that I needed to work at become something more, and that I could only become more if I really worked at it. I prayed a lot, trying to figure out where I was going. I found a group that was very supportive, and this group allowed me to find new interests and talents that I never had considered before. This poem is the inspiration for this book, and I hope that I can help you find your passion, to grow into a positive person, and accomplish all you want to be.

Included in this book are Biblical passages that have helped me, and a section in each chapter called Things to Think About. Also included is a lined page at the end of each chapter for personal reflection on the questions in Things to Think About. Use this section to consider the various thoughts you have had while reading this book.

Personal Stories

I was born in 1971, and had normal development up until I was 2 ½ years old. In 1973 I was in an automobile accident with my parents and two older sisters. I flew through the windshield when a dump truck rear-ended the car we were in. I sustained a closed-head injury, later reclassified as a traumatic brain injury (TBI). I was in a coma for three weeks, and during that time I died three times. During those three times, I was told by God to go back. It wasn't my time to leave this world. After coming out of the coma, I had to relearn how to walk, talk, and many other skills that most take for granted.

The following year, 1974, I was outside with my family at my grandparent's house. We were standing near a fence and gate that looked very similar. My sisters climbed over the fence to go play in the pasture. I wanted to do what they were doing. I didn't realize that what I was climbing on was not a part of the fence, but rather the gate. As I began climbing the gate, the gate fell over. I was underneath the gate. I had a stomach blockage as a result. Not long after that I had to have surgery to correct the blockage because I was unable to keep any food down. I had become malnourished.

Then, when I was 4, because of the doctors not knowing exactly how much I could learn, or even if I could eventually live an independent life, I began going to a special school for learning-disabled children. It was there that I learned how to read.

In 1976, I began kindergarten at a public school. There were several area schools in my town—two public, and one parochial. I began at a public school, and for the first few weeks I went there. At some point, however, the teacher thought I would do better at the parochial school, so I transferred there. Even though I liked the school, it was difficult for me to make friends because I had not begun school there at the beginning of the school year. All the girls in my class already had made friends. I was the new kid, the oddball, and I didn't have any friends that were girls. I became friends with two boys in my class who were in the same boat I was—they didn't have many friends—but they were accepting of me. Even though they were my friends, I still developed depression because I wanted to be accepted by the girls in my class. The boys were my friends for about 4 years, and when some new students came to our school, I befriended these new students because I did not want them to feel the same rejection that I felt when I transferred over. The next few years were pretty decent because I had two close girlfriends.

In seventh grade, I had two major problems come up (at least to a seventh grader). I started arguing with one of these friends, and we grew apart for a long time. Many years later, in 2017, she and I rekindled our friendship. Another major issue was the fact that someone began bullying me. I had been attending school with this girl since I transferred over in kindergarten. My academic progress was on time but still slow. She picked on me because I had difficulty keeping up with the class and understanding the material. She did not know that I was staying up till 11 each night just to get all my homework done. As a result of this bullying, I developed anxiety issues, and 35 years later I still cannot go near that classroom without getting extremely anxious. I transferred to a small country school the following year just so I wouldn't have to deal with the drama anymore.

I returned to the parochial school in ninth grade. My girlfriends had transferred to the public high school, so I had no friends in my class. Fortunately, there were two upper classmen who became friends of mine, and they were very accepting of me. After they graduated, however, I had to figure out a way to make friends. I got involved in a youth group that had many people from around the diocese that helped plan and facilitate youth events within the diocese. I stayed involved with this group for several years because I felt accepted by my peers in the group. My opinion mattered. It felt good to know that they did not think that I was unable or incapable of contributing anything of value to the group. It was in this group that I finally decided I wanted to do more in life, to help others in a meaningful way. But first I had to graduate from high school and get into college.

My junior year of high school I realized that I would be heading out into the real world rather soon. I had no idea if I was even capable of going to college. Midway through my junior year I found out that my overall average was just barely passing. I knew I had to do better than just a 70 to graduate, so I decided I had better buckle down. I had to improve my grades. At the end of my senior year, I had brought my overall average from 70 to 79, all in 1 ½ years' time (yes, I wonder what I could have done if I had come to the realization during my freshman year)! I was accepted into a college just a couple of hours away, but on academic probation. I was there for a school year when I was kicked out of school for lack of academic improvement.

After getting kicked out of school for lack of academic progress, I moved back home, but I still didn't know what I wanted to do. My future seemed bleak. I began arguing with my parents about rules I considered unfair. They kicked me out of the house but had lined up a living arrangement so that I could move in with an aunt two hours away. After living with my aunt for a year (during which I started my academic career over), I moved into my own apartment. I lived there for 2 ½ years. By the end of this time, I had broken up with the person I had dated since high school and began dating the man who would later become my first husband.

During that first marriage, I had several issues come up that I had never experienced before—I was physically and emotionally abused, depressed that I was unable to keep my husband happy, in addition to feeling abandoned. After 13 years of marriage (16 years altogether), I got divorced. I soon started dating again and soon remarried.

The second marriage was ok for a while, and my husband was supportive when I got fired from my job in retail. He suggested I go back to school. I had my BA in psychology, so the next step was to get a masters degree. The marriage was going great until after I graduated. Then I began working an hour away, and my children from the first marriage began to get verbally and physically abused. After nearly 6 years of marriage, we divorced because I refused to raise my children in an abusive environment. My children are very important to me, and I made myself a promise years before that I would never allow my children or myself to be in another abusive relationship, no matter how I felt about the person.

After this divorce, I became extremely depressed, and I didn't like being alone. Even though I had three children at home with me, I was lonely. I needed some adult conversation. I turned to an online dating service, which was a big mistake, as the person I thought I was getting to know scammed me. He made me feel that he loved me, and I spent 1 ½ years talking to the person, and wound up in jail for several months that year because of him. During that time in jail, I turned my life around. I renewed my faith, prayed daily, and found that I needed to stay positive while spending time in jail. I began writing this book while in jail because I knew if I could stay positive, that others could benefit from my experience as well.

Another person who has had great struggles in his life is a close friend of mine. Not long after he was born, he began being physically abused. In addition to physical abuse, because he was not this man's child, the stepfather began injecting him with female hormones. He became a sex slave to his stepfather's friends. He then was forced into a life of drugs, all before the age of 13. At the age of 13, he became a father, but the child was given up for adoption. He then stole a vehicle and wound up in prison for two years, most of it in solitary confinement. The vehicle he had stolen was wrecked, and he sustained internal injuries along with sustaining a traumatic brain injury. When he was released from jail, he moved to another state with another relative, so fortunately the abuse ended. He received his high school diploma, and then took care of his relative till her death, when he was 20. Since jail, he has made a positive change in his life. He is no longer doing drugs, and he has been doing positive things in his life, like helping others do their errands, helping people through their struggles, and so on. However, life has thrown more challenges his way. He has had health issues because of the forms of abuse, and the wreck he was in. He has only one kidney now, and has had cancer as well. While he struggles with these issues, he still tries to be a positive influence in other peoples' lives.

Biblical Study

Struggles often come about because we lack the faith that everything will turn out the way it is supposed to. We attempt to control the situation, rather than allowing God to take control and lead us on His path. The difficulties we face help us to become stronger and wiser as well as building our personal endurance and confidence. That endurance is equivalent to building hope, which is the key to staying mentally strong and positive.

Here are several Biblical passages that help us to become more hopeful and building our self-confidence:

> *Jeremiah 29:10-13 (NIV) This is what the Lord says: "When seventy years are completed for Babylon, I will come to you and fulfill my good promise to bring you back to this place. For I know the plans I have for you," declares the Lord, "plans to prosper you and not harm you, plans to give you hope and a future. Then you will call on me, and I will listen to you. You will seek me and find me when you seek me with all your heart."*

> *Mark 5:24-34 (NIV) A large crowd followed and pressed around him. And a woman was there who had been subject to bleeding for twelve years. She*

had suffered a great deal under the care of many doctors and had spent all she had, yet instead of getting better she grew worse. When she heard about Jesus, she came up behind him in the crowd and touched his cloak, because she thought, "If I just touch his clothes, I will be healed." Immediately her bleeding stopped and she felt in her body that she was freed from her suffering. At once Jesus realized that power had gone out of him. He turned around in the crowd and asked, "Who touched my clothes?"

"You see the people crowding against you," his disciples answered, "and yet you can ask 'Who touched me?'"

But Jesus kept looking around to see who had done it. Then the woman, knowing what had happened to her, came and fell at his feet and, trembling with fear, told him the whole truth. He said to her, "Daughter, your faith has healed you. Go in peace and be freed from your suffering."

Romans 15:1-7 (NIV) We who are strong ought to bear with the failings of the weak and not to please ourselves. Each of us should please our neighbors for their good, to build them up. For even Christ did not please himself but, as it is written: "The insults of those who insult you have fallen on me." For everything that was written to teach us, so that through the endurance taught in the Scriptures and the encouragement they provide might have hope. May the God who gives endurance and encouragement give you the same attitude of mind toward each other that Christ Jesus had, so that with one mind and one voice you may glorify the God and Father of our Lord Jesus Christ. Accept one another, then, just as Christ accepted you, in order to bring praise to God.

Romans 15:13 (NIV) May the God of Hope fill you with all joy and peace as you trust in him, so that you may overflow with hope by the power of the Holy Spirit.

Things to Think About

Have you had struggles that really made you wonder if you could stay positive? What has happened in your life, your personal story, to make you question how you can stay positive? Facing challenges head-on is important because, once faced, your self-confidence will increase and you will feel better about yourself. You will then be able to face other challenges and be able to maintain a positive attitude.

Positivity Defined

Positivity is more than just an attitude. It is a change in the way we live, and involves many aspects: positive thinking, perseverance, determination, belief that things will be alright no matter what, imaging positive living and consequences, courage, confidence, and believing in yourself. One cannot be a positive person without the belief that no matter what happens, things will turn out alright. This sounds simple enough, but it is not easy to maintain. It takes a lot of work to stay positive because people and situations can happen that will bring us down.

Have I ever had a negative thought? Of course! But once I have a negative thought, I remember the struggles that I have already been through, and know that I can get past whatever struggles I am currently going through. What do I do to get through the challenges? I pray a lot and work at changing my mindset.

Positivity includes prayer, attitude, love for self and others, perspective, and caring. I have had many times that, although I prayed, loved, and cared, my perspective was wrong and my attitude was sour. Nothing positive came about until my perspective changed.

Some time ago, I had a legal situation come up, and one of my sisters offered to take in all three of my children even though she has three children of her own, including a special needs child. I became very depressed. Around this same time, my mom was put in hospice care, so there were many things that I had no control over. My anxiety and depression got really high, and I discussed my options with my doctor. He was able to get me on some medication to help with the issues that I was having. Unfortunately, not long after my mom died, I was arrested and spent several months in jail. Although I am generally a positive person, I felt my light had completely burned out, that there was nothing left of me. During my incarceration, I had to change my mindset. I had to begin relying on others to bring me food, medication, and anything else I needed. This was particularly difficult because I have always been an independent person, trying to always be able to rely on myself. I had to learn to rely on my three sisters to take care of things that I could not do while in jail, including my children, financial needs, and meet with my attorney when necessary. This was not easy for me. I began reading my Bible, and also began writing this book.

During this time, I also learned who my true friends were. Although I appreciated my sisters' love and support, I relied heavily on three close friends to keep me going, to give me hope. One of these friends came to visit frequently, usually every other week, but sometimes more often. My other friends in my support system were unable to visit, but we wrote to each other often. I came to rely on their words of encouragement. Another thing I did was pray daily, and read the Bible daily as well. The day I was released from jail, I had been praying especially hard, reading various verses from the Bible that gave me hope. The difficult times, the struggles that have occurred in my life, have been hard to deal with, but I am thankful for those times because they have helped me grow into a more understanding person.

Life is never easy, much as we would like it to be. I am fully aware of this through the challenges I have faced—a traumatic brain injury that resulted in a learning disability, having to relearn how to walk, talk, and function, stomach surgery, emotional problems, and abuse that came from others in my childhood and adult life. Being a slow learner, not being accepted by others, and being bullied were very difficult for a child to go through, especially one who was very sensitive to her environment. Fortunately, through all these bad experiences, I was able to learn how to treat others. I know that I like to be treated in a loving manner, that acceptance is a very important need, and I like to think that I have been able to show others that they are important to me. In the Gospel of John, we are told to "Love each other as I have loved you. Greater love has no one than this, that he lay own his life for his friends" (John 15: 12-13, NIV). Just a little further in the same chapter (John 15:17, NIV), John states it quite plainly: "Love each other." Plain and simple. If we love ourselves and those around us, accept ourselves and others, then we will be less likely to have a negative mindset.

There are many aspects to a positive mindset, and I will cover each of these in depth in the rest of this book. What are these aspects that I believe are most important? First, we must have a purpose, a meaning. Next, we must believe in ourselves, and have courage to take on our daily challenges and goals, as well as conquer our fears. Third, in deciding to work toward our goals, we need perseverance, which is the summation of determination and endurance. Another part of this positive attitude includes gratitude/thankfulness. Finally, prayer and encouragement from yourself and others, particularly friends, is essential. I believe that prayer is more essential, though, because when we believe in something greater than us, it helps us to focus on our strengths. I will go over each of these in detail throughout the book.

Biblical Study

There are several Bible verses that kept me hopeful while in jail. These verses also helped me feel less alone. They are as follows:

> *Psalm 102:1-2 (NIV); Hear my prayer, O Lord; let my cry for help come to you. Do not hide your face from me when I am in distress. Turn your ear to me; when I call, answer me quickly.*

God listens to you when you struggle, and he will guide you when you need help.

> *Psalm 142 (NIV); I cry out to my Lord; I lift up my voice to the Lord for mercy. I pour out my complaint before him, before him I tell my trouble. When my spirit grows faint within me, it is you who know my way. In the path where I walk men have hidden a*

> *snare for me. Look to my right and see; no one is concerned for me. I have no refuge; no one cares for my life. I cry to you, o Lord; I say, "You are my refuge, my portion in the land of the living." Listen to my cry, for I am in desparate need; rescue me from those who pursue me, for they are too strong for me. Set me free from my prison, that I may praise your name. Then the righteous will gather about me because of your goodness to me.*

What this verse told me is that God will help me in times of trouble, that he will be there to listen and to guide me when I am struggling. This, in turn, told me that there is hope in each struggle.

> *Isaiah 40:29-31 (NIV); He gives strength to the weary and increases the power of the weak. Even youths grow tired and weary, and young men stumble and fall; but those who hope with the Lord will renew their strength. They will soar on wings like eagles; they will run and not grow weary; they will walk and not be faint.*

God gives strength to us as long as we trust in him. He will guide us on the path to him, and when we go astray, he will help us get back on track, even though it may take longer to get where he wants us.

> *Isaiah 41:13 (NIV); For I am the Lord, your God, who takes hold of your right hand and says to you, "Do not fear, I will help you."*

God is always with us. We have no reason to fear.

> *Isaiah 42:16 (NIV); I will lead the blind by ways they have not known, along unfamiliar paths I will guide them; I will turn the darkness into light before them and make the rough paces smooth. These are the things I will do; I will not forsake them.*

Deuteronomy 31:8 (NIV); The Lord himself goes before you and will be with you; he will never leave you nor forsake you. Do not be afraid; do not be discouraged.

Isaiah 12:3 (NIV) With joy you will draw water from the wells of salvation.

Romans 12:2 (NIV) Do not conform to the pattern of this world, but be transformed by the renewing of your mind. Then you will be able to test and approve what God's will is—his good, pleasing and perfect will.

Ephesians 4:21-23 (NIV)

When you heard about Christ and were taught in him in accordance with the truth that is in Jesus. You were taught, with regard to your former way of life, to put off your old self, which is being corrupted by its deceitful desires; to be made new in the attitude of your minds; and to put on the new self, created to be like God in true righteousness and holiness.

Philippians 4:8 (NIV) Finally, brothers and sisters, whatever is true, whatever is noble, whatever is right, whatever is pure, whatever is lovely, whatever is admirable—if anything is excellent or praiseworthy—think about such things.

Philippians 4:10-13 (NIV) I rejoiced greatly in the Lord that at last you renewed your concern for me. Indeed, you were concerned, but you had no opportunity to show it. I am not saying this because I am in need, for I have learned to be content whatever the circumstances. I know what it is to be in need, and I know what it is to have plenty. I have learned the secret of being content in any and every situation, whether well fed or hungry, whether in living in plenty or in want. I can do all this through him who gives me strength.

Things to Think About

What needs to happen in your life to bring about a positive attitude? Be specific! What can you do to bring about this change, because it is truly in your hands? What can you do to maintain this attitude? What will it take, long-term, to be positive and to overcome the challenges you have in your life? It may help you to write down your personal goals and ways to achieve them.

Purpose, Motivation, Faith, and Belief

Every single being, whether plant, animal, insect, or human, has a purpose. Some are innate purposes, such as a plant giving off oxygen (plants), while others can be to assist others in daily living (service animals, for example). Humans, however, are given the ability to choose what they work on achieving, whether it be a personal goal—learning a new skill—or tackling a difficult task. Insects even have purposes, although I have yet to learn what the purpose of a cock roach or a red wasp is. As a child I asked many times why things happened the way they did. The reason for each event was never fully explained, but I learned that there is a purpose, a reason, behind each event. My survival of events that could have ended my life meant that there was a reason behind my living, and I fully believe that I will live until my purpose, whatever it may be, is complete.

We all have meaning and purpose! Purpose can be difficult to find. Many times, we see our purpose as being a student, a child, a parent, or an employee. We don't see that we are more than just a role. Yes, you might be any number of these roles, but there is still more to what you can do in your life. You are not JUST a parent, or JUST anything! What gives your life personal meaning? I have always enjoyed helping others, listening to those who are struggling to get through life. It is part of who I am, that innate quality that has been part of my life since after the wreck. Listening to others has always given purpose to my life. Essentially, purpose gives you a reason for being.

For many years, I saw my role as a helper, an encourager, a mother, or a teacher. I knew, though, that I was more than these roles, that my life purpose would be much deeper, and could only be achieved through utilizing my gifts of acceptance, understanding, and empathy. In order to fulfill my life purpose, I had to turn to God for His guidance, and I began working toward the purpose he gave me when my life was saved through His intervention. I felt that God had saved my life because He had a greater purpose for me. Writing this book gave me an additional purpose because I was finally able to help others in a bigger way, helping others in a larger way.

Although you have already read my story, there is more to it. After suffering a traumatic brain injury (TBI), I was in a coma for several weeks. During that time, I had three near-death experiences. God told me to go back. Even at the age of 2 1/2 years old, I knew that this meant I had a purpose to fulfill. My parents knew I had a reason for surviving, and made sure I knew it too. I knew even then that I would not die until I fulfilled that purpose. Fifty years later I am still living purposefully as well as working at helping others with life struggles and mental health issues.

My purpose has changed many times over the years, from helping my parents be grateful for the family they had, letting others know that God exists and helps others in their times of need (as a child), and by encouraging my children to be the best they can be at the roles they pursue in life (as an adult). Setting goals and working toward these God-given purposes gives you the strength to achieve that goal. "The thoughts we allow into our minds and the attitudes we choose to have determine whether we have misery or joy" (Meyer, 2015, The Mind Connection, p. 27).

Recently I asked God what His plan was for me. Was it still to become a counselor, or was my purpose changing to something else? While praying that heartfelt prayer, I heard His response. He told me that I would still help others, but that my role would change. I would help those who have no hope. I have considered this response, and believe that my purpose has changed to writing books so I can help as many people as possible.

Finding that purpose is not always easy, but it allows you to use your gifts, your talents, to help the world. One of my sons uses his gift of writing as a sports journalist. Another son utilizes his mechanical gifts while working on cars, and the youngest son is an entrepreneur. These gifts have allowed them to grow more confident, and develop a confidence regarding other challenges that they may face.

I was not always a confident, self-assured person. My struggles with learning kept me from working my hardest in school, and I was unable to gain a positive outlook. I believed I was incapable because of my peers. I know now that I am capable of doing many things that most others believed impossible. "I can do everything through him who gives me strength" (Philippians 4:13, NIV).

Motivation includes the desire to do something, a reason for doing something. What motivates you to do the things you do? My motivation, right now, is my children, but my ongoing motivation is to prove myself to others. Proving myself has always been there because there were many who thought I would never be able to do the things I have done—walk, talk, ride a bicycle, learn. I can't say that it's been easy. Nothing that is worth anything is ever easy. But is accomplishing something worth the work? YES!!! If there is something that you want to accomplish, then you must work toward it. The only way you can achieve that goal is by working at it, believing in yourself, and staying positive!!!!!

Taking a break from life is something we all want to do at some time, just to breathe, to let go and relax. The stress we put ourselves under causes burnout in our daily lives. By taking a breather, we will be able to refocus once we have that fresh perspective. The struggle will still be there upon our return, but our thinking and feelings—our perspective--about the situation have changed, so we are able to focus on finding a real solution to the difficulty. "Sleeping on it" is a smart thing to do because it is during sleep that our subconscious mind figures out the solution to whatever problem we have. Relaxing and not stressing about whatever situation you are in is helpful as well.

Talking to someone can also help us bring new thinking about the difficulty. By taking that much needed break, we are allowing ourselves to step back, not be so close to the situation. By refocusing on the problem/goal, we can take smaller, although just as effective, steps toward the solution.

Accomplishments are important to keep the person positive. Here is a list of my accomplishments, things that I am proud of:

*Being able to drive, having my driver's license

*Graduating from high school, college, and graduate school

*Becoming a mother

*Having friends that are truly valuable to me

*Helping others through writing

What does your list include? Think about all the things that you have done in your life. Make your own list. I bet you will surprise yourself. My motivations were to become the best I could, given the limitations that others gave me. Proving others wrong about me has always been a key part of who I am. Who or what motivates you to become the person you are meant to be?

Faith is also important. Faith is not just a belief in a supreme being. Faith is having complete trust or confidence in someone or something. Faith requires optimism, a positive spirit. Are you fully confident in yourself? Do you trust that others mean well, that others will help you if you are in need? I found out recently that I had more friends than I realized. I had no idea these people even cared about what was going on in my life, so I had not turned to them before. This was a truly big thing for me, knowing there were others, not just the ones I normally talked with, that cared for me. This increased my belief that there are more good people in this world than we think.

Belief in oneself is extremely important in maintaining a positive attitude! Overcoming the academic difficulties was one of those areas where I had to change my attitude. I had to learn to love to learn. I had to improve in the areas that were challenging to me.

By changing my attitude, I was able to find a better way to learn. I realized that my TBI had made it difficult for learning, and I had to find a new way. Getting the same grades that I had in high school was no longer an option. I realized that I could learn the material if I focused on it in a different way. For example, during graduate school, instead of just focusing on the discussion questions, I would read the assigned chapter, highlight, underline, AND take notes! It was a lot of extra work, but it helped me to learn the material better, and my belief in myself increased substantially.

I encourage every one of you to focus on thinking outside the box, to write down the goals that you have so that you can work on each goal. It is not until the goal is written down that we can commit ourselves to it. Put the goal in an area of your house, work, and car so that each time you look up you see the goal and remind yourself that the goal is within reach. Believing that you can and will accomplish that goal is essential to creating a newer and better you!

The Bible is full of passages related to purpose, motivation, faith, and belief. What follows will be a bit more information about each of these topics, as well as biblical passages related to each.

Your life has a purpose! Everything that you have experienced—good and bad—has been a teaching moment. It is through these moments that we learn and grow. I have known for as long as I can remember that I have a purpose, and that my purpose is to help others. But what do we do if we do not know what our purpose is? The best thing that I can offer you is this: Figure out what you enjoy doing, and use that action to teach others about it. My skill set includes being empathetic and understanding about what others are going through and writing. Your skill set might include cooking, like my oldest sister, or any other creative endeavor.

Motivation is defined as "the process that initiates, guides, and maintains goal-oriented behaviors (Cherry, K., Motivation: The Driving Force Behind our Actions, verywellmind.com). Motivation can be low or high, intrinsic or extrinsic. High motivation action, at least for me, includes writing and being creative in other ways. A low motivation action would be cleaning. When I was attending college, my motivation was usually been extrinsic in that I always wanted to prove others wrong, prove that I was capable. Your motivation may be something else entirely.

Faith and belief can be very similar. Faith and belief are two words we often associate with trust and confidence. Although these two words can be used interchangeably in some contexts, there are some differences between them based on their meaning and context. The main difference between faith and belief stems from their usage; faith is mostly used to refer to religion, but belief is used in a variety of contexts (https://pediaa.com/difference-between-faith-and-belief/). Faith cannot be proved through evidence, while belief is likely to be proven by facts or reality.

Biblical Study

Purpose

Jeremiah 29:11 (NIV) "For I know the plans I have for you," declares the Lord, "plans to prosper you and not to harm you, plans to give you hope and a future."

Romans 8:28 (NIV)And we know that in all things God works for the good of those who love him, who have been called according to his purpose.

Proverbs 19:21 (ESV) Many are the plans in a person's heart, but it is the Lord's purpose that prevails.

Colossians 1:16 (NIV) For by him all things were created, in heaven and on earth, visible and invisible, whether thrones or dominions or rulers or authorities—all things were created through him and for him.

Motivation

Philippians 4:13 (ESV) I can do all things through him who strengthens me.

Matthew 6:1-4 (ESV) "Beware of practicing your righteousness before other people in order to be seen by them, for then you will have no reward from your Father who is in heaven. "Thus, when you give to the needy, sound no trumpet before you, as the hypocrites do in the synagogues and in the streets, that they may be praised by others. Truly, I say to you, they have received their reward. But when you give to the needy, do not let your left hand know what your right hand is doing, so that your giving may be in secret. And your Father who sees in secret will reward you.

Jeremiah 29:11 (NIV) "For I know the plans I have for you," declares the Lord, "plans to prosper you and not to harm you, plans to give you hope and a future."

Isaiah 41:10 (NIV) So do not fear, for I am with you; do not be dismayed, for I am your God; I will strengthen you and help you, I will uphold you with my righteous right hand.

Faith/Belief

Hebrews 11:1 (NIV) Now faith is confidence in what we hope for and assurance about what we do not see.

Mark 11:22-24 (NIV) "Have faith in God," Jesus answered. Truly I tell you, if anyone says to this mountain, 'go throw yourself into the sea,' and does not doubt in their heart, but believes that what they say will happen, it will be done for them. Therefore

I tell you, whatever you ask in prayer, believe that you have received it, and it will be yours.

Proverbs 3:5-6 (NIV) Trust in the Lord with all your heart and lean not on your own understanding; in all your ways submit to him, and he will make your paths straight.

2 Corinthians 5:7 For we live by faith, not by sight.

Things to Think About

What are your personal and professional goals? What can you do to achieve them? What can you use to motivate yourself to achieve these goals?

Confidence and Courage

Confidence is often difficult to come by because what others have said to us brings us down instead of encouraging us. Confidence can be defined several ways. Confidence is "the quality of being certain of your abilities or of having trust in people, plans, or the future" (https://dictionary.cambridge.org/us/dictionary/english/confidence) Another definition of confidence isa feeling of having little doubt about yourself and your abilities, or a feeling of trust in someone or something (https://dictionary.cambridge.org/us/dictionary/english/confidence) Given these two definitions of confidence, what are some ways that we can build our self-confidence? One way is to learn a new skill. As a child you are constantly learning new things. For example, walking and talking are skills that we normally learn as children. It takes time to learn these skills. Reading as well as writing are other important skills we learn that can help boost our confidence. As we grow older, we try on new skills, such as learning how to ride a bike or playing tunes on the piano. We gain confidence through the repetition of skills.

I like to write. I began writing as a child, first as poems and short stories, and later on while researching various topics. It is a skill that I have learned, but there are certain types of writing that I do better at than others. I am not a good fiction writer, although I love to read a good novel, but I can write an excellent research paper if given a topic. What are some things that you are good at? What are some things you can do well that others may not be aware of?

We gain confidence through repetition of skills. Writing your name could be a big confidence booster if you have never been able to do it before. Writing a paper well would be another way. Even though I know how to write a research paper, I would have difficulty writing, say, a persuasive paper, unless I really knew the topic. What are some things you are good at? What are some things that others do not know that you can do proficiently?

One prayer that many people know is the Serenity Prayer, by Reinhold Niebuhr:

God, grant me the serenity to accept the things I cannot change;

Courage to change the things I can;

And wisdom to know the difference.

Accepting the things one cannot change, things that are out of our control, is one of the most difficult things to abide by. We have no control over how others act or react; the only person we have control over is ourselves. We can learn from these times. A child, for example, has no control over the actions of their parents' actions. One child may have really good parents, parents who are supportive of their children, encouraging their children to learn new things and to be the best they can at the things they learn. Another child may also have parents who are abusive, parents who do not put the interests of the child first. The first example is one who has developed confidence in who he or she is, and is unafraid to try new things. The second example is the child who has no confidence because he has been told over the years that he or she is not good enough. The child likely has had some type of abuse—physical, sexual, mental, or verbal abuse—and feels that they can do nothing right, and tries so hard to be the person the abusive parent wants them to be, but is never enough.

Courage is defined as mental or moral strength to venture, persevere, and withstand danger, fear, or difficulty (https://dictionary.cambridge.org/us/dictionary/english/courage). Courage, then, is confidence in the face of fear. What are times that you felt you lacked the strength to do something but did it anyway? That is courage! I remember a time that I was very timid. I had no confidence whatsoever. However, I got involved in a group that worked on planning spiritual retreats for teenagers and young adults.

This was the beginning of my development into a courageous person, one who felt confident in what she was doing.

A friend of mine went through many years of physical, mental, emotional, sexual, and verbal abuse, as well as neglect by his mother and step-father. He ran away from home several times, joined an organization that his step-father belonged to so he would be accepted by his step-father, and finally wound up in jail for a while when he was a minor. He has since completely changed his life, and although he suffers from PTSD, he is able to live on his own, with a little outside help, because of his physical ailments (having one kidney and several traumatic brain injuries). It has taken courage and inner strength for him to survive, to live, and supportive friends, since his family no longer speaks to him.

There are some passages in the Bible that I have turned to when I have needed encouragement. One of these passages, Philippians 4:13 (NIV), reads "I can do all this through him who gives me strength." I use this passage as a sort of meditation when I am struggling a form of mindfulness. I have had to remind myself many times that although God did not put me into the struggles I have had, that he has given me the courage and strength, as well as the confidence, to get through each difficulty. By writing down the goal that you want to achieve and posting it in places where you will see it will allow you to fully believe it in your heart that you can accomplish it.

Biblical Study

> *Hebrews 10:35-36 (NIV) So do not throw away your confidence; it will be richly rewarded. You need to persevere so that when you have done the will of God, you will receive what he has promised.*
>
> *2 Corinthians 12:9 (NIV) But he said to me, "My grace is sufficient for you, for my power is made perfect in weakness." Therefore I will boast all the*

more gladly about my weaknesses, so that Christ's power may rest on me.

Hebrews 13:6 (NIV) So we say with confidence, "The Lord is my helper; I will not be afraid. What can mere mortals do to me?"

Deuteronomy 31:6-8 (NIV) Be strong and courageous. Do not be afraid or terrified because of them, for the LORD your God goes with you; he will never leave you nor forsake you." Then Moses summoned Joshua and said to him in the presence of all Israel, "Be strong and courageous, for you must go with this people into the land that the LORD swore to their ancestors to give them, and you must divide it among them as their inheritance. The LORD himself goes before you and will be with you; he will never leave you nor forsake you. Do not be afraid; do not be discouraged."

John 14:27 (NIV) Peace I leave with you; my peace I give you. I do not give to you as the world gives. Do not let your hearts be troubled and do not be afraid.

Psalm 27:1 (NIV) The LORD is my light and my salvation— whom shall I fear? The LORD is the stronghold of my life— of whom shall I be afraid?

Psalm 56:3-4 (NIV) When I am afraid, I put my trust in you. In God, whose word I praise— in God, I trust and am not afraid. What can mere mortals do to me?

2 Timothy 1:7 (NIV) For the Spirit God gave us does not make us timid, but gives us power, love, and self-discipline.

Things to Think About

We all experience moments of weakness, times of discouragement. Write down how you feel when you feel weak, and how you feel when you feel empowered and courageous. Think about what it would take to feel empowered and courageous. Internalize that feeling. Work at becoming more. How can you develop that inner strength, that ability to see things in a more positive light?

Perseverance, Determination, Endurance and Patience

Determination is seen as the ability to continue trying to do something, although it is very difficult (dictionary.cambridge.org/dictionary/english/determination). Endurance is the ability to keep doing something difficult, unpleasant, or painful for a long time (dictionary.cambridge.org/dictionary/english/endurance). Patience is seen as the ability to wait, or to continue doing something despite difficulties, or to suffer without complaining or becoming annoyed (dictionary.cambridge.org/dictionary/ english/patience). Perseverance, therefore, is a combination of determination, endurance, and patience, and is defined as continued effort to door achieve something, even when this is difficult or takes a long time (dictionary.cambridge.org/dictionary/English/ perseverance).

Determination + Endurance + Patience = Perseverance

Look at the equation up above. Think about it. Reflect on what it means. How does it relate to positivity? Positivity is more than just a positive attitude. It requires perseverance, which involves determination, endurance, and patience. Although one cannot be positive without the attitude, being positive for any amount of time requires all three of these elements. How is this? Think about it. Determination, which is the quality of being resolute (Random House Dictionary, 1992), is knowing that there is a purpose, and endurance is to continually work toward that purpose or goal. But what about patience? In order to endure, we must be patient in our wait for change. Change does not usually come quickly, especially personal change. More often than not, we fail several times before we succeed at the goal we are working toward.

Those that we associate with, be it friends, family, or coworkers, will not always like to see the change, even if it is a positive one. It is easy to be brought down by others, especially if the change is fairly new. One must work continuously at changing ourselves, at staying positive! It is easy to go the lazy route, to fall into a state of depression, but that hole is difficult to dig oneself out of. It takes perseverance!!!

Growing up was not easy for me. I had begun at the public school but then transferred to the parochial school in town. The most difficult thing about the transfer was that my female classmates had already made friends, so me, being the new kid, had a hard time finding friends. I had few friends growing up, and the first friends that I had were two boys in my class that accepted me. Even though I was happy enough to have some friends, I felt cut off from my peers. Even though I had a loving family, it wasn't enough. I was five years old, and the only people I knew were my parents' friends, and they were nowhere near the age of 5. No one knew how important it was for me to have friends my own age. No one saw the anguish I was going through. I was depressed and anxious, but no one knew because my family had the attitude that however you were feeling, you had to deal with it on your own. I could not express myself because of this attitude. This was difficult because as someone who had a brain injury that made learning difficult, I was still expected to do everything on my own.

During those early years, I continued to hang out with the boys, playing Cops and Robbers and Cowboys and Indians. Yes, it was fun, but they couldn't exactly invite me over to spend the night. Then, around third or fourth grade, a couple of new girls came to school. I knew how hard it was for me as a new kid, so I made sure I became friends with them, let them know that they were accepted by someone. It felt good to finally be friends with girls my own age. Even though it doesn't seem like something that belongs in a chapter on perseverance, it does belong because had I not persevered, I would not have these lifelong friends.

What are the things you have accomplished in life, things that you are proud of, difficulties that you have gotten through? Now, as a brain injury survivor, I have had to relearn many things—walking, talking, breathing—but I have also had to learn new things as well. I had to learn what I was capable of, and for many years I had believed that I was incapable of achieving much beyond the high school education I had. But I tell you this, when you change your attitude, your whole belief system, that is when you can begin to accomplish great things! My whole mission throughout my lifetime has been to prove everyone wrong, to prove that I am a capable person, because I felt that no one else believed in me.

Make a list of your achievements. They can be as small as learning how to ride a bicycle, or large, like starting your own business or going further in your education. Besides the things I had to relearn as a child, my accomplishments include getting my driver's license, graduating from various levels of education (high school, college, graduate school), having/raising three children, and figuring out that I was stronger mentally than I had once believed. I know I have mentioned it earlier, but the one passage from the Bible that I carry in my heart is from Philippians 4:13 (NIV): "I can do everything through him who gives me strength." I truly believe that God has given me the strength to accomplish the many things that I have in life. He will give you the strength to get through the difficulties you have as well. Does God give us the difficulties that we go through? Maybe some of them, but I believe that He also gives us the strength to get through them. He guides us so that we can become better people. Often we ask, "Why is God challenging me?" I found the answer in James 1:13-15 (NIV):

When tempted, no one should say, "God is tempting me." For God cannot be tempted by evil, nor does he tempt anyone; but each one is tempted when, by his own evil desire, he is dragged away and enticed. Then, after desire has been conceived, it gives birth to sin; and win, when it is full-grown, gives birth to death.

So, what does this mean? Temptation does not come from God. Unhealthy desire—addiction, lust, gluttony--and temptation come from the devil. Envy is one of the seven deadly sins, and it is also focused on in the Ten Commandments— "You shall not covet your neighbor or his belongings" (Exodus 20:17, NIV). One thing I firmly believe is that although God does not put us into the struggles we have, that he helps us to work through the struggles to get us where He wants us to be.

Perseverance, as noted earlier, is necessary in order to learn to maintain a positive outlook. Have no doubt—there are many times that I wondered why I was going through the difficulties that I went through. I now realize that these were the difficulties I chose, and that God had guided me through the difficulties to get where I needed to be in life. But through each difficulty I learned something new. I persevered because I knew it was part of the big purpose that I had in life. I truly believe that the devil put the tests, the challenges, in my way, and God helped me through them so that I could learn from these challenges. One personal example is the loneliness I went through as a newly divorced woman. I did not feel that I could make it on my own, and here I was with three young children, and struggling to figure things out on my own. I got involved with someone online (big mistake, by the way), and even though I was able to take care of my children, I had to rely on my oldest son to take care of the two younger ones. He let me know if the others were getting into trouble, or had gone off somewhere that they weren't supposed to be. One time, my middle son took off with two older boys to go skateboarding an hour away. They were several years older. Fortunately, I was able to go find my middle son and take him to a trusted relative's house while I went back to work until midnight. God is with me in even the most challenging times, letting me know that He will give me the courage and strength to get through each challenge. He will teach me what He wants me to know. **EVERY CHALLENGE IS A LEARNING EXPERIENCE!!!**

Patience is another lesson to be learned in life. It is through learning patience that we realize that many of the things we want are not always possible right away. We have to be patient in order to get to each goal. Getting an education is a good example of how to learn patience. So is becoming a parent. If we do not have the patience, then we cannot be fully prepared when the time comes for us to become a parent. It takes nine months for the woman to go through a pregnancy. In each of those months we are preparing in a different way, so that we can be fully ready by the time the infant arrives. It is much the same way when you are attempting to accomplish other goals as well. We must develop patience so that we can be fully ready for whatever we have to face.

One thing I always wanted but was discouraged from looking for in life was acceptance. For as long as I can remember, acceptance is the one thing I have always craved, always needed more than anything. As a teen/young adult, I had this, but was discouraged by family because they didn't believe I could truly know what I wanted or needed. So, I eventually broke up with this person. Both he and I have each been divorced twice. Two years ago, he and I found each other again, and the first time we saw each other after, as we hugged each other, I felt all my brokenness come back together. Twenty-nine years later we found our way back to each other. This is what I mean by patience, knowing what is needed and healing the way you need in order to find what you truly need.

Biblical Study

There are many biblical passages related to determination, endurance, patience, and perseverance. Among them are:

> *Philippians 4:13 (NIV) I can do all this through him who gives me strength.*

> *1 Corinthians 15:58 (NIV) Therefore, my dear brothers and sisters, stand firm. Let nothing move you. Always give yourselves fully to the work of the Lord, because you know that your labor in the Lord is not in vain.*

James 1:12 (NIV) Blessed is the one who perseveres under trial because, having stood the test, that person will receive the crown of life that the Lord has promised to those who love him.

Galatians 6:9 (NIV) Let us not become weary in doing good, for at the proper time we will reap a harvest if we do not give up.

Romans 5:3-4 (NIV) Not only so, but we also glory in our sufferings, because we know that suffering produces perseverance; perseverance, character; and character, hope.

Isaiah 40:31 (NIV) But those who hope in the Lord will renew their strength. They will soar on wings like eagles; they will run and not grow weary; they will walk and not be faint.

1 Corinthians 9:24 (NIV) Do you not know that in a race all the runners run, but only one gets the prize? Run in such a way as to get the prize.

James 1:2-4 (NIV) Consider it pure joy, my brothers and sisters, whenever you face trials of many kinds, because you know that the testing of your faith produces perseverance. Let perseverance finish its work so that you may be mature and complete, not lacking anything.

Romans 12:12 (NIV) Be joyful in hope, patient in affliction, faithful in prayer.

Colossians 3:12 (NIV) Therefore, as God's chosen people, holy and dearly loved, clothe yourselves with compassion, kindness, humility, gentleness and patience.

Things to Think About

Last chapter we spoke about courage. This chapter has been about perseverance and how it relates to having a positive attitude. Perseverance utilizes our courage by setting the tone in our focus. What will we focus on and work toward? What are those goals? How can you persevere? How will you be courageous and face those who doubt you and your capabilities? How will you endure the challenges that you face, and get past the ugliness of other peoples' beliefs about you? How can you prove them wrong?

Despair hit me hard.

I had nowhere else to turn.

My only hope

Lay in my belief

That everything would turn out alright.

After I gave up,

I turned my head to pray.

I asked God why he was allowing

So much pain in my life.

He replied, "It wasn't my giving you the pain.

I just gave you

The strength to get past it."

I understood then

That it wasn't God

That challenged me.

It was God who gave me

The strength to endure

Each challenge

The devil had brought

Upon me.

God gave me the ability

To get past each challenge,

Each dare that the devil sent,

So that I could remain

In His grace.

Conquering Fear

It is utterly difficult to conquer a fear, especially if we do not understand where it came from. I did not understand for many years where my own fears, my own inadequacies, came from. Sometimes the basis is a truly traumatic experience, such as abuse, but often it comes from our anxieties, our fears of the unknown. What are the experiences you have kept in your heart, those things that have kept you from moving forward? <u>Each person in your circle of family and friends experiences the same things differently.</u>

My parents, two older sisters, and I all were in a wreck when I was very young. Even though we were all in the same wreck, we all had different experiences, so each of us has had some insight into what happened, but we only are able to understand it from our individual points of view. While I experienced being in a coma for three weeks and several near death experiences, my parents and sisters each had a different experience. My oldest sister had cuts that became scars on her face that she eventually had surgically removed. My parents, who were likely still grieving the loss of their only son four years prior to the wreck, were wondering if they were about to experience a death of another child. My mother carried guilt in her heart because she nearly lost me. My father, on the other hand, was the backbone of the family. He made sure that once we were home from the hospital that Mom stayed busy so that she would not carry the burden constantly. We all knew, growing up, that she was depressed. It took her several years to get past the feelings that she was having. We received different types of support from our parents, and we were able to thrive, even with all the trials our family went through.

What are your fears? Let me tell you about my fears. Normally I would tell you that I have no fears, but that would be a bold-faced lie. My main fear is that I will never find someone who will love me for the person I am. I experienced true acceptance one time in my life—and that relationship was discouraged by my family because they did not truly get to know him. However, many years later, after both of us experienced two divorces each, have found our way back to each other. The first time he and I saw each other again, after an absence of 29 years, he and I hugged each other for what was probably 2-3 minutes, and I felt like all the hurt and heartache that I had experienced since then completely healed inside of me. He and I are still together, and do not plan on being apart again. Even if this relationship does not work out, this will be the last one for each of us.

I have experienced many relationships over the years, and I found that many of these relationships ended because of a "new" discovery about me. Love and acceptance is such an important need. Love and acceptance are important to the human spirit. A lack of love and acceptance makes us believe that we are nothing, that we have no value. **THIS IS NOT TRUE!!!!!** We are all important in different respects, but if we do not know what love and acceptance is, we grow fearful of never experiencing the love that we need to thrive. Who are the ones that love and accept you? Is it conditional or unconditional? Unconditional love, agape, is what we all crave, but few will experience it.

I thought, with each relationship I had, that I had the love and acceptance I desired. I guess I had it for a little while, but it was a fleeting experience, one that was not permanently affixed to the relationship. I have love and acceptance from several friends, but what I have craved is to have that love and acceptance on a more personal, more intimate, level. Will I even have what I so desperately want? I have hope. There is one person who I have always had that more personal, intimate acceptance that I have always craved, and fortunately we were able to find our way back to each other after twenty-nine years apart. What is it that you need in order to feel complete, fully together? Acceptance is what I have always needed. Think about your needs.

Biblical Study

Fear is something that can be overwhelming at times and can bring about anxiety because we do not know how to cope with it. However, I have found that prayer can help me to get past the fear because I put God in control. By taking away the personal focus and allowing my brain to rest, I am allowing my subconscious to work on the solution. There are many biblical verses that focus on fear, which I will now share.

Psalm 34:4 (NIV) "I sought the Lord, and he answered me; he delivered me from all my fears."

Isaiah 41:10 (NIV) So do not fear, for I am with you; do not be dismayed, for I am your God. I will strengthen you and help you; I will uphold you with my righteous right hand.

Psalm 46:1 (NIV) God is our refuge and strength, an ever-present help in trouble.

2 Timothy 1:7 (NIV) For God has not given us a spirit of fear, but of power and of love and of a sound mind.

Matthew 6:34 (NIV) "Therefore do not worry about tomorrow, for tomorrow will worry about itself. Each day has enough trouble of its own."

Philippians 4:6-7 (NIV) "Do not be anxious about anything, but in every situation, by prayer and petition, with thanksgiving, present your requests to God. And the peace of God, which transcends all understanding, will guard your hearts and your minds in Christ Jesus."

1 Peter 5:7 (NIV) Cast all your anxiety on him because he cares for you.

Things to Think About

Make a list of your fears. Think about what it would take to overcome these fears. My biggest fear is spending my life alone and lonely. In order to get past this fear, I have to go out and socialize. I have to make the effort to meet new people, find others who share similar interests, but I also need to socialize with those who make me think about why I feel the way that I do. Write down your fears and work on them. Take them one at a time and work on them. Ask yourself why you feel the way you do. Reflect on why these fears came about. By understanding where the fears all began, you will be able to deal effectively with whatever the difficulty is. However, don't overwhelm yourself with trying to overcome every fear at once. Deal with one or two problems at a time. Figure out what you want, and practice the new behavior until it becomes second nature to you.

Gratitude and Thankfulness

Thankfulness for the things that have occurred in your life, both good and bad, is necessary if you wish to stay positive. Although the US celebrates thankfulness once a year (Thanksgiving Day, in November), thankfulness should be part of our daily lives. We offer thanks when we are given something, and we offer prayers of thanksgiving when we have gotten through a particularly difficult time. We thank those who have been there for us in our times of need. Gratitude is an ongoing thankfulness for our struggles and good times, and we grow from all these experiences.

Most people believe gratitude and thankfulness are the same thing. I believed it myself, until I read something that changed my mind. The Orthodox Christian Network (www.myocn.net) explains it this way: "Gratitude is a feeling whereas thanksgiving is more of an action" (www.myocn.net). One can feel gratefulness without thanksgiving, but thanksgiving is gratitude in action (www.myocn.net). Gratitude is the "manifestation of love, devotion, and commitment towards those who mean the world to you. It encompasses shared experiences, shared love and an understanding that the universe has conspired to keep us happy, and help us under-stand how connected we are to others" (www.graceofgratitude.com).

Being thankful for the things you have endured is a major part of staying positive. I have learned this attitude of thankfulness from my parents, but I could have just as easily learned it from others. They had experienced many challenges even before I was born (military life, raising several children, facing the death of a child), and they were thankful for having survived the worst they could imagine. Then, 2 ½ years after I was born, they nearly lost me. Even though they were still grieving over the loss of their son, they were also grateful that my sisters and I had survived. The guilt they must have felt for feeling joy that their other children survived while their only son had not must have been immense!

Thankfulness is a very important part of keeping positive. I know it sounds contradictory, but be thankful even during the worst of times, the struggles, because those are the times that make us stronger. Those are the times that make us into the people we are. Without the struggles—the brain injury, the mental and physical abuse, and the struggles to raise my boys into the good young men that they have become—I would not have become the hopeful person that I am today. Being thankful for what I have gone through, no matter how big or small, means that I am getting closer to my goal, my purpose in life, which is to help you.

I give you this challenge. Take out a piece of paper and write down the highlights and the downfalls of your life so far. On another sheet of paper write down the lessons you have learned from each of these negative and positive times. My list includes:

    a) Academic struggles due to my head injury—that I am capable
    b) Loneliness—that being alone and being lonely are not the same
    c) Being bullied—that I have value
    d) Discovering that I like helping others—that helping others leads to meaning
    e) Various people who are no longer in my life—certain people are only here for a season, while others are here for a lifetime
    f) The abuse I went through—that I can be alone and feel good about myself and learn to trust others again
    g) The encouragement from others when I felt I could do no more—feeling gratitude for those who helped me
    h) My children—that love comes in all forms
    i) Those that are still in my life despite what I have put them through—that life is not the same without others

I could go on and on, but you get the picture. Write down the lesson that each struggle or joy taught you. Now, after looking over these two papers, think about the strength you developed through this struggles and joys. That should make you smile, because you know that you made it through the tough times, you survived, and you know you can tackle more difficulties as they come. If one can smile at the struggles, be thankful for the difficulties they went through, then the person can maintain a positive attitude. You may be down about a current situation, or the original struggle, but looking at the end result of the previous struggles allows you to know that you truly can get through the worst of times and survive! **YOU CAN GET THROUGH IT!** Each struggle we go through gives us more inner strength, more vitality, and a greater ability to cope with difficulties.

Biblical Study

Gratitude and thankfulness are vital in our lives because without them there is no growth. I'm thankful for the challenges I have been through because without these challenges I wouldn't have learned what I am capable of. The relationships I have had have helped me feel more secure in the person I have become. Although I went through emotional abuse, I am thankful that each struggle built me into the person I am today.

> *1 Thessalonians 5:18 (NIV) Give thanks in all circumstances; for this is the will of God in Christ Jesus for you.*
>
> *Psalm 100:4 (NIV) Enter his gates with thanksgiving and his courts with praise; give thanks to him and praise his name.*
>
> *Philippians 4:6 (NIV) Do not be anxious about anything, but in every situation, by prayer and petition, with thanksgiving, present your requests to God.*

Colossians 3:15 (NIV) Let the peace of Christ rule in your hearts, since as members of one body you were called to peace. And be thankful.

Colossians 3:17 (NIV) And whatever you do, whether in word or deed, do it all in the name of the Lord Jesus, giving thanks to God the Father through him.

Colossians 4:2 (NIV) Devote yourselves to prayer, being watchful and thankful.

Things to Think About

What are you thankful for? Make a list of these things. By making this list you will see the positive things in your life, even in being thankful for bad experiences that taught you something about yourself. I am grateful for the life experiences I have had because I would not be the person I am today. Who are you? What have you learned from? Be thankful for your life and be thankful for the ability to think, dream, and conquer! You can conquer the worst that life throws at you!

The Search for Meaning in Life

What is the meaning of life? I have found that meaning occurs via the situation that we are in. The meaning of the situation as it pertains to our own lives gives us an understanding of life from the perspective that we experience it. As stated in the last chapter, no two people experience the same situation in the same way. We are all different in the ways our mind works and processes the situations we are in. Because of my brain injury, my brain is constantly in the fight or flight mode. My sisters don't understand that this is why I react first rather than think first like they do. We need to learn lessons from the life we are given. I truly believe that all of life is a learning experience. Yes, we may experience bad things, difficult situations, or even blessings in our lives, but each of these experiences is something to learn from.

Like most people, I have struggled with the meaning of life. I finally figured something out, though. Life means something when we have a purpose. Having a purpose begins with what we feel we are being called to do, setting goals, and working to get there. Setting those goals and working toward them gives us something tangible that we can achieve. Years ago, I had no idea what I wanted to do with my life. I wanted to write, maybe become a news reporter, but a teacher told me that I did not have the ability to write like that. This hurt immensely, but I took that information and started looking at things I was good at. Many years later, I found out that I was able to write well after all, and even went so far as to make excellent grades on the long research papers I wrote in graduate school. This experience made me realize that writing related to mental health and positivity would be ways that I could help others. Helping others throughout my life, including many times in primary school, brought satisfaction, especially since I was able to bring hope into the hearts of others. The satisfaction I feel when I am done writing a chapter, or accomplishing something I never believed I could do, brings about feelings of wonder, knowing that I am proving myself capable yet again.

How could I begin to get to where I would be helping others as a career? I began by setting my goal at getting a college education. This would be a struggle because I did not do as well academically as others in my class. I found that I loved psychology. I loved learning how the brain worked in relation to human behavior and mental health. Of course, part of it had to do with the fact that I had a brain injury early on. This led to a fascination of how the brain works.

Setting my goal on a college education was only the beginning. My parents believed that all four of us girls needed to get at least one year of college. My first year didn't count for much, so I restarted my education when I moved to Austin. I retook all the courses, and while it took me 4 ½ years to get my associates degree, it was only 1 ½ years later that I had my BA. After that, my education got put on hold because I got married, had three children, and was working with my husband to help his business grow. We got a divorce after 13 years of marriage, and soon thereafter I found someone who encouraged me to go back to school, so I put forth my effort into getting my masters' degree. I finally was able to work toward my goal instead of encouraging someone else to pursue their goals. Having a goal, a purpose, gives us hope, gives us something to believe in, and gives us meaning.

Hope is the belief that although bad things may happen, that there will be an end to the bad in our lives, that there will be a time that good conquers evil and that good things will embrace us once again. My mother was a truly hopeful person, even through her many years of depression. Although she had lost a son, she did not lose any other children, and was happy to have the children that she had. She knew that God gave her the strength to get through the struggles that she had been through, and she passed that belief onto her daughters and all those she dealt with daily. She was always talking to others, helping them through tough times. She knew that she would not always struggle through life, and she was the model of strength in my life. Her strength and understanding got me through the difficult times, especially when I felt that life was being unkind, and when it was dark.

Much like hope gives rein to positive thoughts, despair gives us negative thoughts. Despair occurs when a person is so low that death is almost welcome. Despair was something I experienced for most of 2018, but while I was in jail, I worked at writing this book and reading the Bible.

You, the reader, are likely suffering from despair, trying to figure out a way to get out of the rut you are in. You feel that your future is bleak, that there is nothing left. Believe it or not, there is light at the end of this tunnel of life. THERE IS HOPE! I have had many times where I felt death was the only option, but I can tell you that the worst feeling is knowing what I would be putting my children through if I left this world by my own hand. They would believe that I was a coward, that I never loved them, or that I didn't love them enough to live. Knowing what I would put them through made me stop and rethink what I was going through.

A friend of mine experienced horrific abuse growing up—physical, mental, emotional, and sexual. His step-father injected him with all sorts of drugs, and prostituted him to adults when my friend was just a child. Because of all these abuses, he developed PTSD, is gun shy about opening up to others, and is close to very few. His surviving family has disowned him, and he has very rarely felt real love. He is sensitive to others, compassionate, and empathetic, yet he feels that he does not know how to love.

I created two little equations:

Purpose + Value = Meaning

and

Love from others + Self love + Spiritual love = Value

Meaning is derived from our purpose and the value we give ourselves. Value is derived from several types of love: Love from others, self-love, and spiritual love. Love from others is what we all desire. It makes life more fulfilling when we have someone to share love with. Self-love is accepting yourself as you are, and if there are areas of your life that you do not care for, you have the courage to make the changes to become what you truly want to be. Spiritual love refers to "a love that is rooted in or supported by a deep spiritual connection that helps us find meaning in life" (www.thriveworks.com/blog/Whatisaspirituallove). Essentially, it is the feeling of being a soulmate, a relationship that is a deep connection with someone.

> As we walk through the fog of life
>
> We can barely see what is in front of us.
>
> We work through the struggles
>
> Much like the sun works to break through the fog.
>
> We carefully walk through it,
>
> But failing to take a chance
>
> Is something we should not consider.
>
> We should take the chance
>
> That life will become better!
>
> Taking that chance creates something new
>
> Within us!

We are here to be the sunshine in other's lives. That is our purpose, our meaning. Someone may be helping you through the fog of life, while you are helping someone else through their fog! Be their light!

Love and acceptance helps us stay positive. Knowing that we matter to others, our valuing others, and loving both others and ourselves is vital to finding meaning and staying positive.

What is love? Love is acceptance of another, even if we are wronged by the person. Love is explained best by St. Paul in 1 Corinthians 13 (NIV). Essentially, if we have gifts of the spirit but do not love, we have given nothing of ourselves. Love is defined here as patience and kindness, and protects, trust, hopes, and perseveres.

Although loving your neighbor is very important, so is love of yourself. We have been told to love our neighbor as we love ourselves. In other words, we cannot love others unless we love ourselves. Love and acceptance from others does help us to acquire a positive attitude, but in order to maintain that positive attitude, we must be able to love and accept ourselves as we are, even with our own personal limitations. When we love ourselves, we open ourselves up to being loved by others, and are more able to love others ourselves. That is pretty deep if you ask me. So, work at loving yourself as you are, and improve the areas that can be improved upon. By doing this, you will be able to accept others more fully.

Biblical Study

> *Jeremiah 1:5 (NIV) Before I formed you in the womb I knew you, before you were born I set you apart; I appointed you as a prophet to the nations.*
>
> *Romans 12:2 (NIV) Do not conform to the pattern of this world, but be transformed by the renewing of your mind. Then you will be able to test and approve what God's will is—his good, pleasing and perfect will.*
>
> *John 8:12 (NIV) When Jesus spoke again to the people, he said, "I am the light of the world.*

Whoever follows me will never walk in darkness, but will have the light of life."

John 14:6 (NIV) Jesus answered, "I am the way and the truth and the life. No one comes to the Father except through me."

Micah 6:8 (NIV) He has shown you, O mortal, what is good. And what does the Lord require of you? To act justly and to love mercy and to walk humbly with your God.

Ecclesiastes 12:13-14 (NIV) Now all has been heard; here is the conclusion of the matter: Fear God and keep his commandments, for this is the duty of mankind. For God will bring every deed into judgment, including every hidden thing, whether it is good or evil.

1 Thessalonians 5:16-18 (NIV) Rejoice always, pray continually, give thanks in all circumstances for this is God's will for you in Christ Jesus.

Things to Think About

Purpose brings meaning to our lives. What do you see your purpose as being? What can you do to fulfill that purpose? How can you show others that you love yourself, but not in an egocentric manner? Are there things that you can work on accepting about you so that you can become open to your God-given purpose?

Negative Thinking

One saying that I have heard many times is this: "Whether you think you can, or you think you can't, you're right" (Henry Ford, 1947). I sincerely believe this, but many times we are unable to see the good in a bad situation. Earlier I spoke about how it is necessary to have a goal to work toward in order to stay positive. However, this is not always good if the goal is set too high. One must set the goals to levels that are a challenge but attainable at the same time. Getting out of your comfort zone is important because it shows you what you can do. Set the goal high, but break it down into more manageable goals. Setting those more manageable goals and achieving them will allow you to feel accomplished when you are still working toward that large goal.

How did I get past the negative thinking? For years I had thought that it was next to impossible to get anywhere in life, but once I began graduate school, which is something I had wanted to do for many years, I was able to focus both on the big goal—the Master's degree—and then break it down into smaller, more attainable goals. I knew the big goal was out there, but I broke it down into goals that were easier to achieve—each quarter I took one or two courses. I then broke it down even further, into what I had to do each week to get through the quarter. It kept me organized, and I knew what I had to work on each week. Knowing what we have accomplished allows us to feel good about ourselves, thereby keeping us positive. The negative thoughts may still be there on occasion, such as when we get frustrated that something is not going as well as we would like as quickly as we want. But then we have to remind ourselves of how far we have come. We cannot continue to live in the past since we cannot change the past, but we can live in the present, and if there is something we want to change in our lives, then we should not be afraid to do it. Our future can be changed. We do not have to live with the mistakes we have made in the past for forever. I do understand how mistakes can haunt a person for a while, but work at proving that you are more than the mistakes you made, work at becoming a better person, and eventually others will see that you are a different person than you were at the time of the mistake.

What is Negative Thinking? And why is it in a book about Positivity?

The topic of negative thinking is in this book because it impacts the way we face challenges. Several decades ago, I suffered from a negative mindset. I was always questioning why I went through the wreck, feeling very different from my classmates, and just trying to figure out why I had so many difficulties with my brain and behavior. My parents had a rule that all four of us girls had to go to college for at least one year but then my mom changed the rule for me because she was uncertain that I could make it in college because of my learning disability. Instead of being required to go to college for a year, she said that I only had to attend a trade school for one semester. This hurt immensely because I felt that she did not believe that I was capable of attending college. It took me several years, but I did finally get several degrees, an associates degree, a BA, and an MS, all in the field of psychology, proving to many that I was very capable. It took me many years, until I was in 11th grade, to figure out that yes, I was going to get into college, and yes, I was going to make a difference in this world. I "pulled my bootstraps up" and studied more effectively, bringing my grades up from a 70 average to a 79 average in 1 ½ years' time. Was it easy? No way! Was it worth it? Most definitely, because I finally saw what I was capable of. Believe me, if I can change my mindset, you can too!

"Negative thinking is not defined as having a few negative thoughts; instead, it refers to a negative thinking pattern about your surroundings and yourself. Many times it's the same, repetitive negative thoughts that keep repeatedly surfacing, day in and day out. Feeling sad or upset about particular things that happen in life is normal, but the continual negative thinking needs attention, and you want to gain control of it to improve your mental health" (Kraft, K. (2025), https://www.powerofpositivity.com/negative-thinking-mental-health/). Negative thinking exacerbates mental health issues if they are already present and can also cause mental illness. Not everyone who engages in negative thinking has a mental illness. Still, it's crucial to have the knowledge and awareness that it can bring about a diagnosable mental illness, and when mental health issues are present, it will only make them worse (Kraft, K., 2025)

Aaron Beck, MD, the founder of cognitive psychology, studied those who were depressed and found that this population had negative thoughts automatically. He found that the negative thoughts "affected overall happiness and mental health and even caused his patients' depression. He noticed that their negative, distorted thinking fell into three categories: negative ideas about themselves, the world, and the future. He called these thoughts automatic negative thoughts (ANTs)" (Alban, D., 2024, Automatic Negative Thoughts (ANTS): How to Break the Habit, https://bebrainfit.com/automatic-negative-thoughts/). The Human Condition Team (THC Team (2023), Automatic Negative Thoughts: What They are, Causes, and How to Overcome Them, https//thehumancondition.com/automatic-negative-thoughts/)
found that there are several causes/risk factors of ANTs, including life stressors, personality traits, maladaptive perfectionism, self-critical thinking style, and adverse childhood experiences.

ANTs can really have a negative effect on the human body. First, they deplete the feel-good neurotransmitters serotonin and dopamine. They slow the production of brain-derived neurotrophic factor (BDNF), which is a protein needed for the formation of new brain cells. Next, the size of the brain shrinks, while the amygdala (the brain's fear center) enlarges. The risk of psychiatric and neurodegenerative diseases increases. Finally, ANTs also accelerate the aging process of the brain, so these psychiatric and neurodegenerative diseases are likely to be seen earlier (Alban, D.,

2024). The THC team found that there are many possible impacts of ANTs including an increase in both depressive symptoms and anxiety, decreased motivation, emotional and behavioral changes, and reduced success, hope, and resilience (THC Team, 2023).

Finally, the THC Team found that there are many treatments that can be considered in the person who has automatic negative thoughts. Professionally, the patient/client can be treated with a) Cognitive Behavioral Therapy (CBT), b) Mindfulness-Based Cognitive Therapy (MBCT), c) Acceptance and Commitment Therapy (ACT), d) Transactional Analysis (TA), and e) Positive Psychotherapy. (THC Team, 2023). For those who feel self-help is the best way for treatment, there are also many interventions that can be utilized. They include: a) Self-compassion, b) Self-acceptance, c) Mindfulness-based interventions, d) Psychoeducation and Bibliotherapy, e) Journaling, f) Breathwork, g) Emotional self-care, h) Social connectedness, and i) Medication (THC Team, 2023).

What are the negative thought patterns that we need to watch out for? Alban (2024) found that there are nine particular automatic negative thought patterns that we need to be aware of in ourselves. Black and white thinking includes using words like "always," "never," and "every." Focusing on the negative instead of the positive is another roadblock many of us have. Fortune telling and mind reading are also considered negative thought patterns. Fortune telling includes thinking about the worst-case scenario and believing that will happen. Mind reading occurs when you assume what someone else believes. Thinking with your feelings "occurs when you have negative feelings without questioning them" (Alban, 2024). "Being ruled by the shoulds" (Alban, 2024) is something most of us do. I should have done this instead of that. These shoulds make us feel stupid, like we can't do anything right. Then there is labeling. Labeling occurs when we call ourselves or others degrading things, such as stupid, fat, ignorant, or anything that makes us or the other person feel unworthy or small. Taking things personally happens a lot!!! Think about it. You want someone particular to know how you feel, but then when you try to tell them, they blow you off. You haven't done anything to them, and you don't know what has been happening in their day-to-day life. They snapped at you and you take it personally, and it makes you feel like poo. But the best thing you can do for yourself is not take it personally, realize that just maybe they have been having a bad day. The last negative thought pattern is blame. It could be self-blame or blaming someone else for an event (Alban, 2024).

Is there a way to change the negative thoughts?

Alban (2024) discusses how to challenge automatic negative thoughts. The first way is to ask yourself these questions: a) Is this thought true? b) Does having this thought serve me? c) Is there another explanation or another way of looking at things? And d) What advice would I give to a friend who had this thought? Another way to challenge your ANTs is to write down your ANTs. While these questions are a good start, here are more questions to ponder while you journal and consider what your negative thoughts do for you. You can do this exercise in your head or by writing down your answers in a journal.

1. Is the thought true? Is there a basis for this negative belief?
2. Is the thought giving you power, or is it taking your power away?
3. Can you put a positive spin on this thought or learn from it?
4. What would your life look like if you didn't have these negative beliefs?
5. Is the thought glossing over an issue that needs addressing? (Smith, E., 2022, What is Negative Thinking? How it Destroys your Mental Health. www.healthyplace.com)

Journaling can help you to understand where the thoughts are coming from. Personify your inner critic. Is it a dragon? Or another type of monster? How does that monster make you feel? What can you do to eliminate the monster, or at least lessen its impact? View your negative thoughts as boring (notice and let it go—a form of mindfulness). This will help you departmentalize your negative thoughts until you are ready to work on them without stress. Turn your ANTs into PETs. PETs are positive empowering thoughts. Reframe "should" and "shouldn't" statements. For example, change "I should be going to the gym" to "I can find an enjoyable exercise that will help me get fit." Meditation is another possible way to challenge your ANTs. How does meditation work? Meditation helps you quiet your mind by using a mindfulness technique: While practicing meditation, one learns to notice and dismiss thoughts, letting them pass by with no emotional investment (Alban, 2024). Finally, practice gratitude. What are some things you are thankful for? "Being grateful reduces negativity by creating a boost of feel-good brain chemicals like serotonin, dopamine, and oxytocin" (Alban, 2024).

Biblical Study

There are so many biblical passages that concern a person's thinking! Ponder the meanings behind each passage as to how it pertains to negative thinking. All of the biblical passages for this chapter are from the NIV interpretation of the Bible.

> *Proverbs 3:5-6 Trust in the Lord with all your heart and lean not on your own understanding; in all your ways submit to him, and he will make your paths straight.*
>
> *Proverbs 4:23 Above all else, guard your heart, for everything you do flows from it.*
>
> *Proverbs 12:18 The words of the reckless pierce like swords, but the tongue of the wise brings healing.*

Joshua 1:9 Have I not commanded you? Be strong and courageous. Do not be afraid, do not be discouraged, for the Lord your God will be with you wherever you go.

Jeremiah 29:11-13 "For I know the plans I have for you", declares the Lord, "plans to prosper you and not to harm you, plans to give you hope and a future. Then you will call on me and come and pray to me, and I will listen to you. You will seek me and find me when you seek me with all your heart."

Isaiah 41:10 So do not fear, for I am with you; do not be dismayed, for I am your God. I will strengthen you and help you; I will uphold you with my righteous right hand.

Psalm 18:16-19 He reached down from on high and took hold of me; he drew me out of deep waters. He rescued me from my powerful enemy, from my foes, who were too strong for me. They confronted me in the day of my disaster, but the Lord was my support.

Romans 12:2 Do not conform to the pattern of this world, but be transformed by the renewing of your mind. Then you will be able to test and approve what God's will is—his good, pleasing and perfect will.

Ephesians 4:29 Do not let any unwholesome talk come out of your mouths, but only what is helpful for building others up according to their needs, that it may benefit those who listen.

Philippians 4:8 Finally, brothers and sisters, whatever is true, whatever is noble, whatever is right, whatever is pure, whatever is lovely, whatever is admirable—if anything is excellent or praiseworthy—think about such things.

James 3:5-6 Likewise, the tongue is a small part of the body, but it makes great boasts. Consider what a great forest is set on ire by a small spark. The tongue also is a fire, a world of evil among the parts of the body. It corrupts the whole body, sets the whole course of one's life on fire, and is itself set on fire by hell.

James 3:14-15 But if you harbor bitter envy and selfish ambition in your hearts, do not boast about or deny the truth. Such "wisdom" does not come down from heaven but is earthly, unspiritual, demonic.

1 Peter 2:1 Therefore, rid yourselves of all malice and all deceit, hypocrisy, envy, and slander of every kind.

Things to Think About

What can you do to keep negativity out of your life? Are there situations or people who are toxic to you, people who don't believe in you and what you want in life? Do you need to omit people or situations from your life? Do you need to add other things to your life to become a better person?

Prayer

What is prayer? Prayer is communication, a way to talk with God or whatever spiritual being that you believe in. "Prayer is primarily seen as a two-way dialogue between you and God. It's not just about making requests but expressing gratitude, confessing sins, and simply connecting with God in worship and adoration" (https://www.biblestudytools.com/topical-verses/prayer-bible-verses/). Prayer can be done in many ways: telling God what is going on in your life, the frustrations as well as thankfulness about the difficulties you have been through, and petitioning God for help in getting through a particularly tough time, such as grief.

Does God answer prayers?

Yes, God answers prayers. They may not always be the answers we want, but they are his answers nonetheless. I have two particular times that my prayers were answered in the way I wanted, but the answers that mean the most are the ones where he allows us to learn from whatever situation we are in.

One time, while I was a teenager, my maternal grandmother was living in a little house behind my parents. We knew that this was going to be her last Christmas in the little house because she was about to be admitted in a nursing home about an hour away. She suffered from a form of dementia called Alzheimer's disease. Anyway, I prayed for one last good Christmas, knowing that she would likely not be participating in anymore Christmases much longer. My prayer was answered because she made her German potatoes one last time. Another prayer was answered a year ago. I was working at a fast-food restaurant. The morning I was scheduled to work, I was very anxious about working because I knew I was likely to be working with someone who stressed me. I didn't pray for that person to not work that day, but rather the strength and wisdom to be able to have a peaceful day. When I got to work, however, I found that the person was not working that day. They had called off. Obviously God works in mysterious ways, ways which we do not understand, but he is always watching over us, listening to us, and helping us when we cannot do anything about whatever situation we are in.

Prayer is an important part of staying positive. There are some that may say that prayer is unnecessary, that God does not exist. I am here to tell you that prayer is a very important part of my life, and it has been for as long as I can remember.

There are many reasons to pray: petitions, thankfulness, for others, for ourselves, and even for the world and its leaders. Most of my prayers are for others, but there are times I have asked for inner strength, or guidance, or even thanking God for helping me get through the struggles I have had in life. I recently prayed for patience and understanding so that I could deal with a situation more effectively. Once I put the prayer out there, I was able to let go of the stress that I was feeling. I do believe that prayer helps us because we as individuals are letting go of control of a situation. Trying to control a situation gets us in trouble.

In Rediscover Jesus (Kelly, 2015, 122-123), he devises a prayer process that we can learn a lot from. This 7-step process includes:

a) Gratitude—Thanking God
b) Awareness—Review what happened in the previous 24 hours
c) Significant moments—What is God trying to tell you?
d) Peace—Ask for forgiveness
e) Freedom—How is God inviting you to change your life?
f) Others—Pray for others
g) Pray the Our Father

By doing this prayer process, we can grow more spiritually by making an effort to build a stronger relationship with God. By building this relationship, we become more positive, build upon our faith, begin to hope more, and learn to love ourselves in addition to others, as well as loving God.

One thing I have learned over the years is that God will help you through the struggles that the devil puts in our way. He will give you the endurance you need if you let Him (1 Corinthians 10:13, NIV). Here is a poem I wrote during a particularly tough time:

> Despair hit me hard.
>
> I had nowhere else to turn.
>
> My only hope
>
> Lay in my belief
>
> That everything would turn out alright.
>
> After I gave up,
>
> I turned my head to pray.
>
> I asked God why he was allowing
>
> So much pain in my life.
>
> He replied, "It wasn't my giving you the pain.
>
> I just gave you
>
> The strength to get past it."
>
> I understood then
>
> That it wasn't God
>
> That challenged me.
>
> It was God who gave me
>
> The strength to endure
>
> Each challenge

> The devil had brought
>
> Upon me.
>
> God gave me the ability
>
> To get past each challenge,
>
> Each dare that the devil sent,
>
> So that I could remain
>
> In His grace.

Think about that now. What struggles have you had to endure? That inner strength wasn't just in you. It was given to you from God. He knows what the devil will put you through, and He will not let us go the path alone. We just have to let go of our need to control the situations we are in because each of these situations is a lesson we need to learn. By knowing that God cares about us, and knowing that he will not allow us to be harmed without reason, we can think in a positive manner. We know we will get through the struggles we are in because the struggles we go through are purposeful. This is how we build hope, in our belief system.

Here is another poem I wrote about challenges:

> I woke up this morning
>
> With dread in my head
>
> But I had to relax
>
> And face the day
>
> That lay ahead.
>
> I knew it would be a challenge,
>
> A fight to the end,

But I kept at it

And had hope be my friend.

I conquered the challenge

That the day had brought,

And I am ready to face

The challenge,

The dare,

That each new day brings.

Tomorrow is not promised,

But today I endured,

And if I wake up tomorrow

I know that I can

Face the challenges

That it brings.

Biblical Study

Philippians 4:6 (NIV) Do not be anxious about anything, but in everything by prayer and supplication with thanksgiving let your requests be made known to God.

Mark 11:24 (NIV) Therefore I tell you, whatever you ask in prayer, believe that you have received it, and it will be yours.

Romans 8:26 (NIV) Likewise the Spirit helps us in our weakness. For we do not know what to pray for as we ought, but the Spirit himself intercedes for us with groanings too deep for words.

Matthew 6:6 (NIV) But when you pray, go into your room and shut the door and pray to your Father who is in secret. And your Father who sees in secret will reward you.

Matthew 6:9-13 This, then, is how you should pray:

> "Our Father in heaven,
>
> hallowed be your name,
>
> your kingdom come,
>
> Your will be done,
>
> On earth as it is in heaven.
>
> Give us today our daily bread
>
> And forgive us our debts, as we also have forgiven our debtors.
>
> And lead us not into temptation,
>
> But deliver us from the evil one."

James 5:16 (NIV) Therefore, confess your sins to one another and pray for one another, that you may be healed. The prayer of a righteous person has great power as it is working.

Matthew 26:41 (NIV) Watch and pray that you may not enter into temptation. The spirit indeed is willing, but the flesh is weak."

Colossians 4:2 (NIV) Continue steadfastly in prayer, being watchful in it with thanksgiving.

1 Thessalonians 5:16-18 (NIV) Rejoice always, pray without ceasing, give thanks in all circumstances; for this is the will of God in Christ Jesus for you.

Things to Think About

When there are things going on that we are having problems dealing with, many times we stress and get overwhelmed by situations that are out of our control. It is not worth it to stress over those things because we cannot control the outcome of the situation, so we need to turn it over to God. Prayer is important because it helps us to refocus, to realign our thinking from negative to positive. We see possibilities that we never saw before! This is how prayer works!

Love and Acceptance

Over the years I have taken to studying many theorists in the field of psychology. Two of my favorite psychological theorists are Abraham Maslow and Erik Erikson.

Abraham Maslow developed the hierarchy of needs. The hierarchy of needs contains five levels of needs that each person has. The five levels are: a) Physiological needs, b) Safety and security, c) Love and belongingness, d) Self-esteem, and e) Self-actualization. The hierarchy of needs is usually displayed as a pyramid of needs, each building on top of the previous needs, as seen in the picture below. Physiological needs include food, clothing, and warmth, while safety and security includes shelter as well as work. Love and acceptance (belongingness) includes relationships with others. Self-esteem pertains to the mental health of the individual, such as confidence, achievements, and feeling like you are a productive member of society. Self-actualization is the complete realization of one's potential, and the full development of one's abilities and appreciation for life. Self-actualization is seen at the top of Maslow's hierarchy of needs, so many may not achieve this need, although we will all work toward it (Perera, Ayesh, 2024. Self0Actualization in Psychology: Theory, Examples, and Characteristics. www.simplypsychology.org'self- actualization.html).

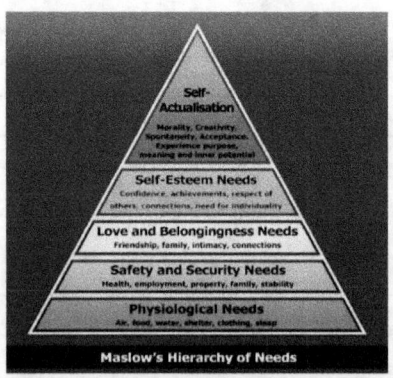

https://librarymonday.blogspot.com/2021/12/maslows-hierarchy-of-needs-worksheet.html

Another theorist, Erik Erikson, developed a theory of psychosocial development that ranges the entire theoretical lifespan of the individual. These eight stages are crises that we each go through in different times of our lives. These eight stages include:

a) Trust vs. mistrust
b) Autonomy vs. shame and doubt
c) Initiative vs. guilt
d) Industry vs. inferiority
e) Identity and repudiation vs. identity diffusion
f) Intimacy and solidarity vs. isolation
g) Generativity vs. self-absorption
h) Integrity vs. despair (P. H. Miller, 1989, p. 178).

These stages are important because if we go through a stage such as trust versus mistrust, and we do not develop a trust in our parent/caregiver, we will have a difficult time developing trust in others later on in life. This does not mean that we will never be able to develop trust, but that it will likely be more difficult to develop trust.

As you can see in the above list, there is both a positive and negative aspect to each stage of development. If the person develops the negative trait, mistrust in this example, the person is likely to develop a pessimistic outlook in life, whereas the person who develops the positive aspect of trust will have a more positive outlook. Can these outlooks change? Most definitely. These are not set in stone. For example, I had a fairly positive outlook on life, but there were situations I was in during my first and second marriages that brought about a negative outlook. I developed mistrust, shame and doubt, guilt, inferiority, and isolation because what I expected to come about in marriage was not a part of the equation. Have I changed? Yes, some. Although I still have some of these aspects of negativity, things have gotten better. Although I still live by myself, I am not as isolated as I once was. I have learned to believe in myself again. These negative aspects will always be a part of my life, but I can improve, just like you can.

Erikson's sixth stage, intimacy vs. isolation, coincides with Maslow's stage of love and belongingness. We learn how to be in relationships of all kinds and will either develop socially or isolate ourselves. As you can see, it is very important to develop social relationships because without them we are more likely to develop mental health disorders such as social anxiety, depression, and generalized anxiety disorder, as well as other mental health conditions.

The next level is safety, such as shelter. Third is the level of love and belonging. Love and belongingness is extremely important because it is through our relationships with others that we learn who we are, and what is important to us individually. To have a positive development psychologically, we must love and accept ourselves. Although it helps most of us if we have family or friends that love and accept us, we must first love and accept ourselves! This can be very difficult, especially if all we see are the imperfections and not our strengths. The last two levels include esteem needs, and self-actualization. These really cannot be met unless we have the sense of love and belonging, so even though they are equally important to the mental development of the individual, I find that love and belonging are the most import-ant part of the equation of mental health.

Why is love and acceptance so important? It is because when we are loved and accepted by others, we find that we think more positively. I was in jail recently, and my cellmate was a bit of a pessimist. Me being a generally positive person, I had a tough time with her as a cell-mate. I asked to be put in a single cell because I felt that it was the only way I could stay in a positive mindset. Her life experience was completely different than mine, and I could see how it made her develop the negative mindset that she had. Whereas I saw my time in jail as a time that I needed to think and reflect about my life, come to some decisions about my children, she saw that all she had done was suffer in life, and she couldn't see anything positive about life. The only day I saw a sincere, happy smile, was the day she got released from jail.

Over the years I have had varying degrees of love and acceptance from family and friends. I have finally concluded that if I am not loved and accepted by certain people, that I will look for love and acceptance elsewhere. My friends have become more like family than those in my "real" family. I have worked hard at becoming a good person, a positive example for my children (even with being in jail). Does that mean that I was jolly the entire time I was there? No way! There were many times that I was down, that I had a difficult time dealing with my emotions, but for the most part I was positive. I knew that the devil had pushed me into the position I was in, but God was helping me through it by giving me the inner strength. I could not have gotten through the time in jail without God or the friends who wrote or came to visit. Those friends got me through the worst of times. That is why love and acceptance is so important! Without love and acceptance, we are unable to develop into the person we are meant to become. Without God, we will struggle. With God, we will push through the struggle and win the battle.

Here is a poem I wrote about friends during that challenging time:

> Friends are there
>
> In your time of need,
>
> To be supportive,
>
> To show you that
>
> You can get through
>
> The worst of times,
>
> To bring you up
>
> When you are down.

I felt so lonely

For so long,

But I found

That I needed

To be a friend

To others

To find the people

I needed in my life.

There are no regrets now

Because I have found

Those that will be here

For me.

Biblical Study

Acceptance

John 6:37 (NIV) All that the Father gives me will come to me, and whoever comes to me I will never cast out.

Galatians 3:28 (NIV) There is neither Jew nor Greek, there is neither slave nor free, there is no male and female, for you are all one in Christ Jesus.

Acts 10:34-35 (NIV) So Peter opened his mouth and said: 'Truly I understand that God shows no partiality, but in every nation anyone who fears him and does what is right is acceptable to him.

1 Peter 3:8 (NIV) Finally, all of you, have unity of mind, sympathy, brotherly love, a tender heart, and a humble mind.

Love

Romans 12:9-11 (NIV) Love must be sincere. Hate what is evil; cling to what is good. Be devoted to one another in love. Honor one another above yourselves. Never be lacking in zeal, but keep your spiritual fervor, serving the Lord.

Romans 13:8-10 (NIV) Let no debt remain outstanding, except the continuing debt to love one another, for whoever loves others has fulfilled the law. The commandments, "You shall not commit adultery," "You shall not murder," "You shall not steal," "You shall not covet," and whatever other command there may be, are summed up in this one command: "Love your neighbor as yourself." Love does no harm to a neighbor. Therefore love is the fulfillment of the law.

> *John 13:34-35 (NIV) A new command I give you: Love one another. As I have loved you, so you must love one another. By this everyone will know that you are my disciples, if you love one another.*
>
> *1 Corinthians 13:1-13 (NIV) If I speak in the tongues of men or of angels, but do not have love, I am only a resounding gong or a clanging cymbal. If I have the gift of prophecy and can fathom all mysteries and all knowledge, and if I have a faith that can move mountains, but do not have love, I am nothing. If I give all I possess to the poor and give over my body to hardship that I may boast, but do not have love, I gain nothing. Love is patient, love is kind. It does not envy, it does not boast, it is not proud. It does not dishonor others, it is not self-seeking, it is not easily angered, it keeps no record of wrongs. Love does not delight in evil but rejoices with the truth. It always protects, always trusts, always hopes, always perseveres. Love never fails. But where there are prophecies, they will cease; where there are tongues, they will be stilled; where there is knowledge, it will pass away. For we know*

in part and we prophesy in part, but when completeness comes, what is in part disappears. When I was a child, I talked like a child, I thought like a child, I reasoned like a child. When I became a man, I put the ways of childhood behind me. For now we see only a reflection as in a mirror; then we shall see face to face. Now I know in part; then I shall know fully, even as I am fully known. And now these three remain: faith, hope and love. But the greatest of these is love.

Things to Think About

Remember, you must first love and accept yourself as you are before anyone else can. Once you love and accept yourself, you will be more able to love and accept love from others. What can you do in order to bring your own personal love and acceptance into your life? Think about how you can show love and acceptance toward others.

Depression, Anxiety, and Loneliness

Dealing with a mental illness that is caused by a situation such as loneliness is a difficult thing, more so because you are in excruciating mental pain. Loneliness can happen when you are all alone, but more often than not, it happens when you are with those who are supposed to be supportive of you but you don't feel the support that you need. Most recently I have felt this type of loneliness. When I began to write this book, it wasn't so much to help you, my readers, but in order to help myself to overcome a negative situation. I had gotten myself involved in a situation that wound up with me going to jail.

Normally I am a fairly happy person. I deal with most difficulties with ease. But this time I had gotten involved with the wrong person, and it wound up costing me a lot of money, along with relationships with immediate family. We were all going through a difficult time because of our mother's long-term illness, and we knew that her time would be coming soon. We had all dealt with it in our own ways, grieving while she was alive for the most part, although the loss of her physically still hit us hard.

I was dealing with my second divorce during this time, and I was trying to get on with my life. I was dating someone online. I thought I had found the person I wanted to spend my life with. He made me feel secure. But then he began some behaviors I probably should have questioned more, but he said I didn't need to worry, that I would not get arrested or be in jail. That should have been a red flag for me right then, but I had already gotten emotionally involved. I couldn't imagine how anyone would allow another person to get hurt.

The police then came to my house with a search warrant. I didn't know what else to do. I allowed them to search my house. At the same time they reported me to protective services because my house was unsafe for my children to live in, so for the time being my children and I moved in with my father for a month while I got the work done on my house. Prior to the end of this month, though, my younger sister and her husband knew I couldn't afford to take care of my children at that point, and that the police had already come to search my house. They felt that an arrest was inevitable, and they offered for my children to come live with them. The boys moved two hours away from me.

Within a few days I got myself a slightly better job than I had, but with a likely arrest coming up, I felt that I needed the boys to live with my sister and her husband rather than with me. It was one of the saddest times in my life. Even though I had a job to go to every day, I was extremely depressed. I felt I had no purpose. I had one or two friends that I talked to regularly, but it was still a very difficult time because I couldn't see them. Then, at the beginning of the second month, my mother died. The boys had been living away from me for a month now. At this point I guess I could have had them move back in with me, but I did not want to uproot them again. The arrest had still not taken place at this point. Two weeks after my mother's death, the police came to arrest me.

I spent from February 21, until June 6, in jail. The most lonely part about it was that I could only call two of my 3 sisters, and the one I could not call was the one who had my boys. Even though I got letters and cards from my two older sisters each week, it was not as meaningful to me as it should have been. I valued the letters I received from my friends more than my sisters. I felt very lonely. My depression and anxiety were the highest they had ever been. I was suicidal several times, and even attempted to take my life at one point while in jail, but the only thing that stopped me was knowing that my boys would see me as a coward, and the pain and torment that they would go through. I had to change my mindset, really get to thinking about what was going on in my life, and how I was going to change it whenever I got out of jail.

The most discouraging thing about being in jail was that my family would not bond me out so I could attempt to get on with my life. This is one of the many reasons why I was so depressed, and why their letters and cards did not mean as much to me as they should have. I felt that they were writing me out of the guilt they felt for leaving me there. Even though the relationships with my sisters were not the best at this time, we have all gotten somewhat closer since then. During the time I spent in jail I was extremely depressed, so I began reading different parts of the Bible as well as writing this book. I felt that if I could help myself get out of the funk I was in, that maybe this book would help others to stay positive during times of struggle.

Depression, anxiety, and loneliness are common mental health conditions that seem to be common in those who are negative. Many times these conditions can be reduced by changing one's mindset. These conditions have been a part of my life for as long as I can remember, but it wasn't until this year (2018) that I fully realized when they began. There was no one around that knew what I was going through, so I felt isolated. It wasn't until 2018 that I realized that there were actually some people who cared about me. Even though I am still on medication to control the intensity of the anxiety and depression, the loneliness, for the most part, is gone because I know who I can rely on.

Depression and anxiety are afflictions of those who have no hope, who do not know which way to go. I have suffered from these two psychological disorders for many years, but I have also been optimistic for most of my life because of the near death experiences I had as a child. When I was told, even as early as 2 ½ years of age, to go back, I knew that I had a purpose. Even through my most depressing times I knew that God was carrying me through them, that I had a purpose for being, and that I had not fulfilled that purpose yet. I am thankful for the struggles I have been through because they have made me a stronger person. I know that these struggles will help me to help others.

Finding people that have experienced similar things helps to alleviate the loneliness, depression, and anxiety. Meeting with others in a support group allows you to feel less alone, since you are not the only person dealing with an issue. People who understand what you are going through is crucial to your own mental health. Find your purpose. Find hope. Devote yourself to following through on your purpose. By finding something that is fulfilling you are not only helping others but you are also helping yourself. You are able to stay positive. You are able to become a better person.

Mindfulness

Depression, anxiety, and loneliness are all difficult emotions to get through. However, there are many ways to help oneself that you can do almost anywhere in order to get through what is perceived as negative emotions.

Mindfulness is "the practice of observing your experience in a nonjudgmental, compassionate, and accepting manner. It begins with simple awareness, paying attention to your experience from moment to moment" (McKay, Davis, and Fanning, 2011, Thoughts & Feelings, Fourth Edition, p. 115). Mindfulness "has been shown to significantly reduce anxiety and panic, depression, and anger, as well as confusion among cancer patients, and chronic pain. Mindfulness has also been helpful in reducing symptoms of stress, psoriasis, binge eating, and fibromyalgia. Mindfulness is also used as part of the treatment program for worry, phobias, and interpersonal conflict" (McKay, Davis, and Fanning, pp. 115-116). There are many ways to be mindful, including observing your body and observing your thoughts.

Observing your body includes a) mindful breathing, b) breath counting, c) breath labeling, d) body scanning, and e) inner-outer shuttle. The methods I usually use when I am anxious include mindful breathing—taking slow and deep breaths—and breath counting. These methods work because they take your mind off of whatever the worry or thought is. The method of breath labeling is similar to mindful breathing or breath counting, and happens when you say "in" on the inhale, holding for several seconds, and "out" on the exhale, again holding for several seconds. Doing this relaxes your mind and body and helps you to refocus on whatever it is that you are doing.

Body scanning includes becoming aware of how each area of your body feels. To begin body scanning, you need to lay down. Are you cold or warm, tense or relaxed? Notice your thoughts while scanning your body for how each section feels. Are your thoughts negative or positive, or are they kind of just there? Let these thoughts go when you realize how they distracted you from the exercise (McKay, Davis, and Fanning, pp. 118-119).

"Inner-Outer Shuttle is a variation on Body Scanning in which you focus on distinguishing between internal bodily sensations and outside sensory experiences. This will help you become more mindful of your environment and how your body reacts to it" (McKay, Davis, and Fanning, p. 119). While seated, close your eyes and do a body scan, concentrating on how the inside of your body feels. Then, notice how the environment feels against your skin, or whatever you hear. You will alternate "looking inside your body" and then sensing your environment for several minutes (McKay, Davis, and Fanning, p. 119).

Observing your thoughts includes the exercises of White Room, Inner Shuttling, Conveyer Belt, and Wise Mind Diagram. The white room is a place where we go mentally to breathe, observe out thoughts, and let them go. Acknowledge your thoughts, whatever they are, and let them go (McKay, Davis, and Fanning, p. 120).

Inner shuttling is much like the inner-outer shuttle because there is alternating between two perspectives. However, inner shuttling is different in that you will alternate between four aspects: physical sensation and the emotion that you feel with the physical sensation, and then thought and emotion, where you think the thought and then the emotion that comes along with that thought. This exercise helps you to detach your emotions from the physical sensation or thought with whatever emotion you are feeling (McKay, Davis, and Fanning, p.121).

The conveyer belt helps you by "noticing and labeling whatever passes through your mind, as if your mind were a conveyor belt moving from the present into the past. Imagine that you're looking down on a slow conveyor belt that is passing from right to left" (McKay, Davis, and Fanning, p. 121). Visualize the details. Then label whatever comes to mind, whether it is a thought, memory, feeling, or even a regret (McKay, Davis, and Fanning, pp. 121-122).

The wise-mind diagram begins with a section called Wise Mind, the observing self. There are three offshoots to this section: Thoughts, Feelings, and Actions. Consider an emotional event. I will give you a personal example. A couple of years ago I was at my dad's celebrating Christmas. The whole family was there. My sisters and I were preparing dinner, which is quite stressful if you do not have everything timed just right. Anyway, I began getting anxious because everyone else was doing their part, while I had to wait to start mine. I got upset with my sisters because I felt useless and the stress was getting to me. Well, I do not have a car. I was so upset that I began to walk home. My youngest son saw me angrily walking and he came up next to me and talked me down, basically using the Wise Mind method, although it was while talking rather than writing it down. We discussed my thoughts, why I was upset, and why I was running away before we even ate dinner. We discussed my feelings while also considering the actions I had taken (beginning the walk home). He was able to calm me down so that I could actually stay and enjoy the family time.

Other methods of mindfulness that I find helpful when I am depressed or anxious are visualization when I am at work or in another stressful situation, or visualization when I am listening to classical music, which is usually done at home. I frequently do the visualization with classical music at bedtime, when I am trying to relax and wind down for bedtime. I visualize a happy place, such as the mountains or the beach, but you might imagine a park or working in the garden. I believe we all have a "happy place" that we can go to when we are stressed, depressed, anxious, or lonely.

Biblical Study

Mindfulness

Be still before the Lord and wait patiently for him. ~ *Psalm 37:7 (ESV)*

But Jesus often withdrew to lonely places and prayed. ~ *Luke 5:16 (NIV)*

Peace I leave with you; my peace I give to you. Not as the world gives do I give to you. Let not your hearts be troubled, neither let them be afraid. ~ John 14:27 (ESV)

Loneliness

Deuteronomy 31:8 (NIV) The Lord himself goes before you and will be with you; he will never leave you nor forsake you. Do not be afraid; do not be discouraged.

Psalm 23:4 (NIV) Even though I walk through the darkest valley, I will fear no evil, for you are with me; your rod and your staff, they comfort me." –

Psalm 34:18 (NIV) The Lord is close to the brokenhearted and saves those who are crushed in spirit.

Matthew 11:28 (NIV) Come to me, all you who are weary and burdened, and I will give you rest.

Romans 8:38-39 (NIV) For I am convinced that neither death nor life, neither angels nor demons, neither the present nor the future, nor any powers, neither height nor depth, nor anything else in all creation, will be able to separate us from the love of God that is in Christ Jesus our Lord.

Depression

Psalm 34:17-18 (NIV) When the righteous cry for help, the Lord hears and delivers them out of all their troubles. The Lord is near to the brokenhearted and saves the crushed in spirit.

Isaiah 41:10 (NIV) Fear not, for I am with you; be not dismayed, for I am your God; I will strengthen you, I will help you, I will uphold you with my righteous right hand.

Matthew 11:28 (NIV) Come to me, all who labor and are heavy laden, and I will give you rest.

Psalm 143:7-8 (NIV) Answer me quickly, Lord; my spirit fails. Do not hide your face from me or I will be like those who go down to the pit. Let the morning bring me word of your unfailing love, for I have put my trust in you. Show me the way I should go, for to you I entrust my life.

Anxiety

Proverbs 12:25 (NIV) Anxiety weighs down the heart, but a kind word cheers it up.

Matthew 6:34: (NIV) Therefore do not worry about tomorrow, for tomorrow will worry about itself. Each day has enough trouble of its own.

Philippians 4:6-7 (NIV) Do not be anxious about anything, but in every situation, by prayer and petition, with thanksgiving, present your requests to God. And the peace of God, which transcends all understanding, will guard your hearts and your minds in Christ Jesus.

1 Peter 5:7 (NIV) Cast all your anxiety on him because he cares for you.

Things to Think About

Mental illness is a very difficult thing to get past. It happens for many reasons—the way you are treated by others, the way you treat yourself, brain injuries of any sort, because of situations that we go through, or even genetically. Find a purpose and work toward a goal, no matter how small that goal is. Do you want to meet other people? Find a small group to socialize in, to belong to. The group should ideally be something of interest to you. Do you like to read? Join a book club at the local library. Do you like to sew? Advertise your talents! Do you want to learn more about your ancestors? Find a genealogy group! By focusing on an interest and following through, you will find yourself feeling better than you were before. You will still have the mental illness, but by finding something you are interested in, you will be focusing on the interest and not the depression. You will begin feeling better!

Facing Challenges

We each have challenges that we must face in life. Your challenges will not be the same as my challenges. Mine have been primarily mental—a learning disability from a traumatic brain injury, and mental health issues that have been part of my life for as long as I can remember. What has gotten me through most of my difficulties is my faith, but it has helped me to have others around that care for me, my friends that I consider to be even closer to family than I ever knew. I am now closer to family than I ever was before. I write about things that happen in my life, relationships, and things that are important to me. My poetry is an extension of who I am, and helps explain things I am going through in ways I cannot express verbally (All the poetry in this book was written by me in various stages of my life). Forgiveness is something I have had to learn about, and I have forgiven those who have hurt me. It will be a lifelong process because we get hurt mentally and emotionally frequently. Actually, everything that is in this book is a skill I have had to learn. I use them every day!

Having a positive attitude and keeping the positive attitude is easier said than done. You may wake up feeling great, like you can seize the day, that nothing can go wrong, and then hit rock bottom, or you can start out with a really bad day and someone just happens to bless your life with their presence, but your whole attitude changes! Frequently we put all the responsibility on others to keep us positive, and this is not the key to developing our own happiness. The key to your own happiness lies within you! Even if something bad happens, we can keep the positive mindset if we take on the attitude that God (or any other spiritual being) will help us through the trial. We can look at the challenge as learning experience, something for us to get through so we get to where we are supposed to be. I am of Christian belief, so I speak of God.

Some things I have been doing more since 2018 are reading The Bible and also attending church as much as possible. Some verses that have helped me are:

> *"Hear me, O Lord: let my cry for help come to you. Do not hide your face from me when I am in distress. Turn your ear to me; when I call, answer me quickly" (Psalm 102: 1-2, NIV).*

> *"For I am the Lord, your God, who takes hold of your right hand and says to you, do not fear, I will help you (Isaiah 41:13, NIV).*

> *"I can do everything through him who gives me strength" (Philippians 4:13, NIV).*

This particular verse keeps me going at all times, because I know that each difficulty I go through, no matter how large or small, God will help me get through it and give me the strength to endure. Keep this in mind always and a positive mindset will follow!

Two of the greatest challenges we each face is accepting ourselves as we are, and respecting ourselves. If we accept ourselves and our personal limitations, others will see that we have self-respect, and if they are any type of good person, they will respect us as well. How do we respect ourselves? By not allowing others to abuse or bully us, or in the way we react to any given situation. If we know that something in our hearts is wrong, we need to speak up, make our voices be heard. I had little self-respect for many years. I stayed in an abusive marriage, one that made me feel like nothing. I finally came to the realization that I was a capable person, that I could become a better person on my own. After being out of that relationship for many years, I still have tough days. He really did a number on me, but I have been able to become a better person.

Self-confidence is another area where many of us fail. It goes hand-in-hand with self-respect, because if we respect ourselves, our confidence level will rise. Sometimes others will disregard us, making us feel that we don't matter. This tears down the person that we are meant to be, that confident, self-assured person we know we are capable of being. It is extremely difficult to bring that person up from ground zero, because that person has no hope, no goals, and no dreams, and many times that person relies on others to make decisions for them. Self-confidence comes from the realization that you can decide for yourself, you can become better than you ever thought, and that you feel valued.

Struggles are more than the ability to go forward. They are things that we have to overcome to become a better person. They are very personal, and many times these struggles are faced because no one else known about them. Have you ever just listened to a person talk about something that is happening in their life? Sometimes we are able to see things that they cannot see for themselves, and can offer help regarding the situation. Other times we may not be able to offer anything but our ability to listen. By opening up about the struggle you are going through, you are allowing someone else to offer help in ways that may be helpful to you in your personal journey of growth. Too many times we feel that we have to get through the journey alone, but sharing the struggle helps not only you but others as well because when you share the burden with others, the burden is shared by many instead of just one. Think of the Titan god Atlas, whose burden was to carry the heavens on his shoulders for all time after he was defeated by Zeus. He was only one person, and yet he had to carry the weight on his shoulders for all time. This is how it is when we shoulder our challenges by ourselves. By sharing the challenges with our friends or with God, the burden is lessened on our own shoulders.

Forgiveness of self and others is the solution to many problems, but it is only through true forgiveness, which involves a lot of reflecting and consideration about the problem, that we are able to have the load lifted off. I recently had a dilemma that I knew I could not get through on my own. I had been reading the Bible and came across Psalm 130 (NIV), which is about asking for forgiveness. By putting yourself fully into asking forgiveness, you are redeemed. Also, by forgiving those who have hurt you, no matter how long ago, the offense is released from your soul. The shame and doubt that was part of your life because of that particular offense is no longer there. That forgiveness brings peace to your heart. Don't forget the lessons from the difficult times, but rather figure out who you are despite the memories. It took me 35 years to finally forgive someone, but I have finally been able to let it go. I have to remember that I have become a better, more accepting person, because of the wrongs done to me back then.

Biblical Study

Challenges

James 1:2-4 (NIV) Consider it pure joy, my brothers and sisters, whenever you face trials of many kinds, because you know that the testing of your faith produces perseverance. Let perseverance finish its work so that you may be mature and complete, not lacking anything.

2 Corinthians 4:17 (NIV) For our light and momentary troubles are achieving for us an eternal glory that far outweighs them all.

Psalm 34:17-18 (NIV) The righteous cry out, and the Lord hears them; he delivers them from all their troubles. The Lord is close to the brokenhearted and saves those who are crushed in spirit.

Ephesians 6:10-11 (NIV) Finally, be strong in the Lord and in his mighty power. Put on the full armor of God, so that you can take your stand against the devil's schemes.

Things to Think About

Challenges happen in all walks of life. It is only a matter of a different type of challenge for each group. Pray about the challenges you are going through. Let the challenge go up to God, allow Him to take control. By letting go of the challenge, you are not stressing as much as before, and you are thinking more clearly. When you are thinking more clearly, you may all of a sudden think of a workable solution to the challenge you have been facing!

Afterward

Overcoming has been a part of my life for as long as I can remember. No doctor gave my parents any hope for my recovery, but through lots of prayer and hard work, I was able to relearn how to walk and talk, learn in school whatever concepts I needed to learn, by learning that no one is the same, and that we must learn to value and respect the differences among us, Building Hope is as much a book about my struggles as it is about overcoming difficulties in life.

Romans 15:13 (NIV) states something we all need to read and understand: May the God of hope fill you with all joy and peace as you trust in him, so that you may overflow with hope by the power of the Holy Spirit."

I realize many of you have had horrendous things happen to you. I understand that you would rather forget instead of forgive. Remember this, though: You are who you are because you have survived! You have value in this world! Although you would not have chosen to live through the situations that you went through, you survived, and you gained internal strength because of it! You are a survivor! Now you must learn to live, to thrive! You have value, purpose and strength!

I have written many poems over the years, and I recently wrote one after a particularly difficult day.

> I woke up this morning
>
> With dread in my head
>
> But I had to relax
>
> And face the day
>
> That lay ahead.
>
> I knew it would be a challenge,

A fight to the end,

But I kept at it

And had hope be my friend.

I conquered the challenge

That the day had brought,

And I am ready to face

The challenge,

The dare,

That each new day brings.

Tomorrow is not promised,

But today I endured,

And if I wake up tomorrow

I know that I can

Face the challenges

That it brings.

You, dear reader, have the strength to face any challenge you have! I believe in you!!!!

Bibliography

Alban, Deane (2024). Automatic Negative Thoughts (ANTS): How to Break the Habit.

    https://bebrainfit.com/automatic-negative-thoughts/

    www.biblestudytools.com/topical-verses/prayer-bible-verses/

    https://dictionary.cambridge.org/us/dictionary/english

Cherry, Kendra (2023). Motivation: The Driving Force Behind Our Actions.

    https://www.verywelmind..com/what-is-motivation-2795378

    www.graceofgratitude.com

Hasa (2016). Difference Between Faith and Belief.

    https://Pediaa.com/difference-between-faith-and-belief

Kelly, Matthew (2015). Rediscover Jesus. North Palm Beach, FL: Blue Sparrow.

Kraft, Kirstin (2025). Doctor Explains What Negative Thinking Does to Your Brain.

    www.powerofpositivity.com/negative-thinking-mental-health

    https://librarymonday.blogspot.com/2021/12/maslows-hierarchy-of-needs-worksheet.html

McKay, Matthew, Davis, Martha, and Fanning, Patrick (2011). Thoughts & Feelings: Taking Control of Your Moods & Feelings, Fourth Edition. Oakland, CA: New Harbinger Publications.

Meyer, Joyce (2015). The Mind Connection: How the Thoughts You Choose Affect Your Mood,

Behavior, and Decisions. New York: FaithWords.

Miller, Patricia (1989). Theories of Developmental Psychology, Second Edition. New York:

W.H. Freeman and Company.

    www.myocn.net

Random House Dictionary (1992).

The Human Condition Team (2023). Automatic Negative Thoughts: What They Are, Causes, and How to Overcome Them.

    https://thehumancondition.com./automatic-negative-thoughts/

www.ingramcontent.com/pod-product-compliance
Lightning Source LLC
LaVergne TN
LVHW020448070526
838199LV00063B/4876